T0265536

PRAISE FOR *FROM JUST ESTHER TO POLY-ESTHER* AND DR. ESTHER M. ALEGRIA

Heroes are often larger-than-life figures who inspire us but to whom we have difficulty relating. *From Just Esther to Poly-Esther* is a heartwarming and compelling story of how one woman overcame significant educational, language, financial, cultural, and corporate obstacles to become a leader in the life sciences. She did it with tenacity, vision, passion, and humor. *From Just Esther to Poly-Esther* is a must-read for those looking for heroic, but relatable, role models in science and business.

—Maureen K. O'Connor
CEO of ZealCare, Lawyer and Entrepreneur

This life story delineates surprising insights of a life lived with a genuine determination to overcome, succeed, and make a difference. I have known Esther as a colleague and friend. She has molded and impacted the careers of so many through her coaching, example, as well as a contagious energy and zest for life. She has a pragmatic and relatable business sagacity that endears her to those she mentors and allows them to internalize her wisdom into life-long changes. She has been able to blend her scientific acumen with functional business approaches that make learning how she translated enormous challenges into defining business strengths a very worthwhile read.

—Juan Torres, PhD
Former Chief Quality Officer at Biogen

A thought-provoking book written in a style that is not just relatable but authentic. For folks interested in understanding how to build belonging, this book provides a simple and powerful perspective.

—Joydeep Ganguly
Senior Vice President, Gilead Sciences

When you're in the presence of an exemplary leader who brings joy to the workplace, joy to relationships, and joy to life—you're in the presence of a timeless leader. *From Just Esther to Poly-Esther* is about the unique and inspiring journey of a special leader who has conquered life's challenges and gracefully navigated many of its twists and turns. Esther's insights and experiences take you on an unforgettable journey, providing a transformative roadmap for *all* who aspire to achieve greatness with perseverance, hard work, and grit.

—Machelle Sanders
North Carolina Secretary of Commerce

FROM JUST ESTHER TO POLY-ESTHER

ESTHER M.
ALEGRIA, PhD

FROM JUST ESTHER TO POLY- ESTHER

**EMBRACING EVERY PART OF
YOURSELF TO TRANSFORM
YOUR LIFE AND CAREER**

 | Books

Published by Advantage Books, Charleston, South Carolina.
An imprint of Advantage Media.

ADVANTAGE is a registered trademark, and the Advantage colophon is a trademark of Advantage Media Group, Inc.

Printed in the United States of America.

10 9 8 7 6 5 4 3 2 1

ISBN: 978-1-64225-838-7 (Hardcover)
ISBN: 978-1-64225-837-0 (eBook)

Library of Congress Control Number: 2023923741

Cover design by Analisa Smith.
Layout design by Ruthie Wood.

This publication is designed to provide accurate and authoritative information in regard to the subject matter covered. It is sold with the understanding that the publisher is not engaged in rendering legal, accounting, or other professional services. If legal advice or other expert assistance is required, the services of a competent professional person should be sought.

Advantage Books is an imprint of Advantage Media Group. Advantage Media helps busy entrepreneurs, CEOs, and leaders write and publish a book to grow their business and become the authority in their field. Advantage authors comprise an exclusive community of industry professionals, idea-makers, and thought leaders. For more information go to **advantagemedia.com**.

To my husband Carlos, who has brought so much peace into my life and is always ready to support and celebrate anything that happens to me;

To my children, Jesse and Lili, who have always been the light of my eyes and inspiration to be better; And to my grandchildren, Chaz, Jasmine, Carmella, and Orion, who have collectively taught me what a special role it is to be a grandmother.

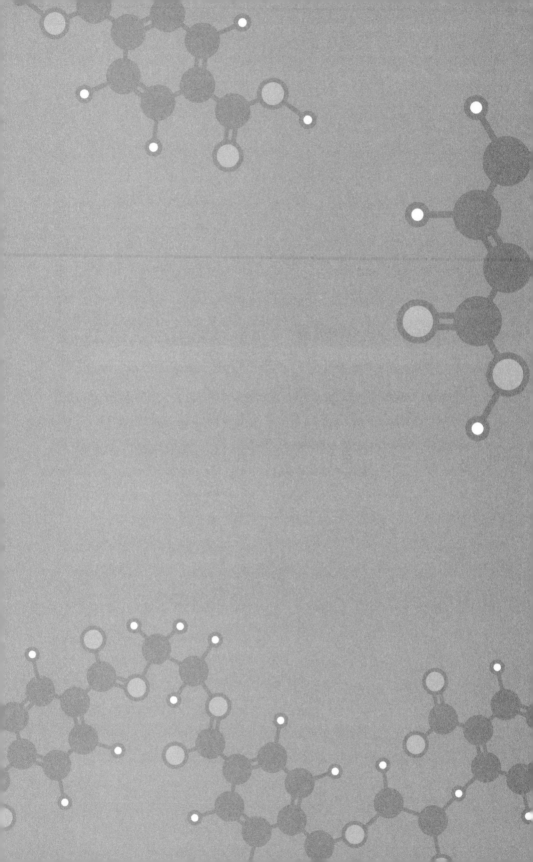

CONTENTS

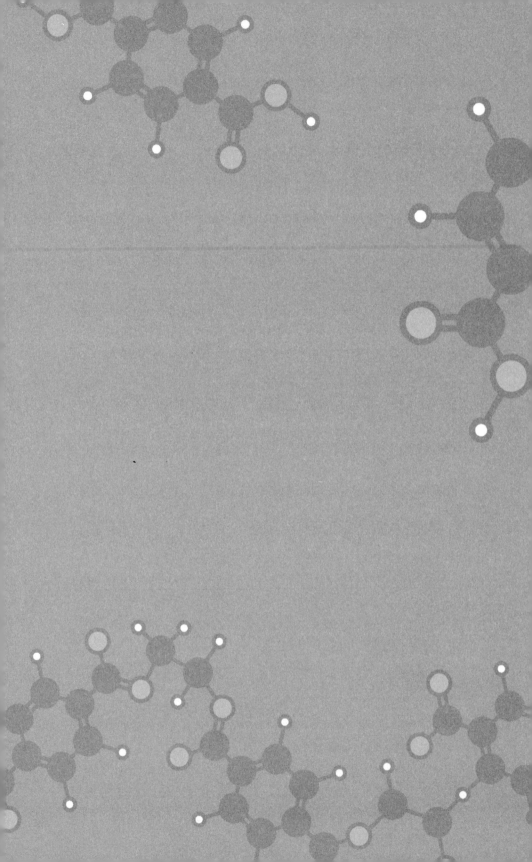

INTRODUCTION

At the age of twenty-four I lived in Fort Bragg, North Carolina. Specifically, my family and I resided in a mobile trailer park close to the military base. We had very little furniture to our name. Our possessions were scarce. And money? We knew what it was. We just didn't have any.

Before the move to the United States, we had lived in several places in Puerto Rico. We were from the island and knew firsthand how hard it was to find work there. During the 1980s, shortly before we left, unemployment rates soared.

Complicating the situation was the fact that we had two young kids, Jesse and Lili. They needed to be fed and clothed. The burden of their livelihoods and future weighed on me every single day.

I also carried something else with me. It was a dream—a big dream. I had earned a two-year college degree in Puerto Rico. The associate degree gave me the credentials to work as a quality control technician in a pharmaceutical plant close to my hometown. While there, I witnessed the introduction of new therapeutic drugs in a way I had never imagined. Suddenly, I was helping to manufacture medications that my family used. My relatives and friends could get relief and healing from work that I was involved in. The experience stuck with me. I wanted to help patients. Moreover, I wanted to *lead* in projects that aimed to improve health outcomes.

Yes, I had a dream. I also had limited education to fulfill my dream. The kind of dream I had would require a PhD in life sciences, plus years of experience in the field. I had none of those. There was no visible path forward in my life at the time.

But I digress. Back to my story on the island. We needed steady work. My husband, at the time, struggled to maintain a suitable position in any line of work. I had to leave my studies at college to take on an entry-level job in Puerto Rico and was the only one bringing in an income to our household. Finding help to care for the kids while I was working was a challenge. It seemed impossible to achieve my dreams. Every day, my goals seemed to drift further and further away.

Then I heard about the army. Through my own research, I saw there could be opportunities in it. By signing up, our family would receive the support we needed. I might be able to study further and pursue a career. I carried out a careful analysis and determined that this option made a lot of sense.

After many discussions, I convinced my husband to enter the army. We sold everything we had in Puerto Rico (not much!) and moved to North Carolina, where he was stationed. We settled into a mobile home trailer park close to base.

That's how I found myself, at the age of twenty-four, adapting to a new culture and language. I didn't know much English at the time. I had a five-year-old, Jesse, and a one-year-old, Lili, who needed constant care. I had to learn words to be able to shop at the grocery store. We had no family or friends in the area when we arrived. I didn't know anyone else. All seemed so different to me, and there was no chance of returning to Puerto Rico, my comfort zone.

And yet, I still had that dream. It would visit me while I slept. Vivid images would flash in my mind. I would see myself dressed well, serving as the director of manufacturing at a pharmaceutical plant. I was in charge of quality assurance. I was working hard to help better the lives of others.

Then I would wake up. I would look around and see our tiny living space. I would remember that I lacked years of schooling, not to mention a couple of degrees. I would see my children and their needs. In an instant, I would be reminded of my immediate responsibilities and reality would hit.

At the time, daily routines and tasks took over. I didn't get the degrees right away. However, I found a way to keep studying. I continued working toward the goal during the years that followed. Eventually (and you'll learn more about this in the chapters to come!) I got that PhD in life sciences.

The achievement opened new opportunities. It gave me the chance to work as a Research & Development scientist in a large biopharmaceutical company. It presented different challenges, which I found I loved. I thrived on delving into these situations and resolving issues at hand. I had the chance to travel the world, meet with medicinal regulatory agencies, and present my research work at conferences. I participated in breakthrough medical advances. I was involved in the development of Prevnar and Meningitec vaccines, working on them from preclinical stages to commercialization. These awesome experiences opened the doors to other opportunities in the industry. I've been given titles including "director," "vice president," "senior vice president," and CEO. My journey has included nonlinear developments, with many chains of events that ultimately built on each other to promote growth in my professional career. You could call me Poly-Esther, as Lili will say.

Through it all, my goals stirred me to continue, to dream even bigger, and to lead with confidence. My passion stemmed from a sense of urgency to achieve a better life for my children and the patients I served.

Today I serve as the chief innovation officer and founder of APIE Therapeutics. My company aims to take systemic sclerosis (aka scleroderma) therapies, as well as for other unmet diseases, from preclinical to clinical trial stages around the world. I am also part of the board of directors for two public companies in the healthcare industry and part of the board of trustees in a life sciences economic development organization. This work aligns with my long-time dream of leading the way toward improved patient outcomes.

What It Takes

Pop quiz: How do you discover and set your goals, get ahead, and enjoy the ride to success?…Even when all seems against you…when you do not have a "godfather" to give you a hand…

If you're searching for the answer, let's talk.

I've often wondered the same thing. Throughout my career's trajectory, I spent many years figuring out how to do so.

Now, looking back, I have stories to share about my journey. In the pages that follow, you'll find my own experiences. Trust me, they are full of turns and twists, of mountains and valleys in the scheme of life. In short, there are many tales that veer away from the "path to success."

Before we get too far, let me assure you of one point. If your life has strayed a bit, that's OK. If you have faced setbacks, don't worry. If you're not sure how to get over the obstacles ahead, you've come to the right place.

I have found there is no linear, continual path to success. And guess what? That's OK and at times necessary. There are many ways to get to the top.

Along the way, life's ups and downs provide valuable lessons. We can learn from our experiences. We're able to analyze and apply new strategies going forward. Facing tough times gives us a chance to build resilience. If we're open, we'll find plenty of opportunities nestled inside of challenges. As my wise mother, also named Esther, often said, "You are the architect of your own destiny."

A dash of creativity and a dose of persistence provide the energy needed for the ride. If we lean into them, they'll drive us forward. When we set our minds and heart to focus on our dreams, the sky is really the limit.

In the chapters of this book, I'll expand on the details. I'll present a clear picture of how my dream turned into a career for me. I'll discuss how I moved up—though bear in mind it was not a straight climb!

There's good news for you, regardless of your current circumstance. If you want a spot at the top, I'll be the first to encourage you to get there. In the following five sections of this book, which are referred to as compounds, we'll explore different aspects that will help you on your own path.

In the first compound, titled "Know Where You're Going," we'll look at the importance of having a goal and keeping the focus on that objective. We'll explore how to find your passion, break through barriers, and set a vision. Throughout the second compound, "Different Is Great," we'll discuss how being different can be great. I'll reflect on times in my own life when I felt completely alone—and yet, having distinct traits ended up being an advantage. It can be like that for you too.

We'll look at persistence in the third compound, "Keep on Knocking on Doors," which outlines the opportunities that can be found with some legwork as an alternative to not having a support group or godfathers. I want to spend some time on ambition too. I'll also discuss why it is essential to maintain integrity. Being ready to push yourself will be the topic of compound four, "Have No Excuses," in which we'll consider the rewards of going out of your comfort zone.

In the fifth and final compound, "Bond with Others," we'll have some fun looking at ways to enjoy every step! Life doesn't have to be dreary. Being willing to laugh at your own mistakes can be the perfect antidote (trust me, I've tried it many times! It works!). Embracing life can lead to days filled with plenty of light, warmth, and good humor.

Through it all, we'll see that there are opportunities to grow at every stage. Just as the twenty-year-old version of me carried herself and made decisions differently than the forty-year-old self did, you may find yourself changing too. That's because we tend to absorb lessons and use them to develop as we go through life. In my case, throw in the personal experiences that I've undergone, and you'll come up with a collection of elements that are now a part of me. Since my daughter coined the term, I have been called "Poly-Esther" many times, and always with a nod to these different roles and attributes. You might become your own version of this concept: Are you a Poly-John? A Poly-Anne? A Poly-George?

Certainly, my journey hasn't been one that would be considered easy by textbook standards—and it's not over yet. I've learned so much along the way; the memories from the hard times keep me balanced as I reflect on the career highs. I've found that having fulfilling, meaningful work has opened my heart to more. I've mentored many up-and-coming leaders and looked after my own family's needs.

And I want to help you too. So let's get started.

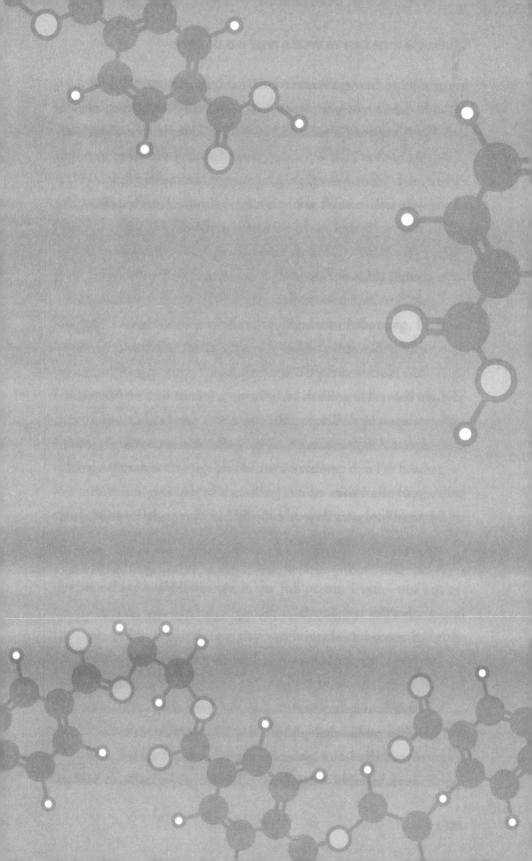

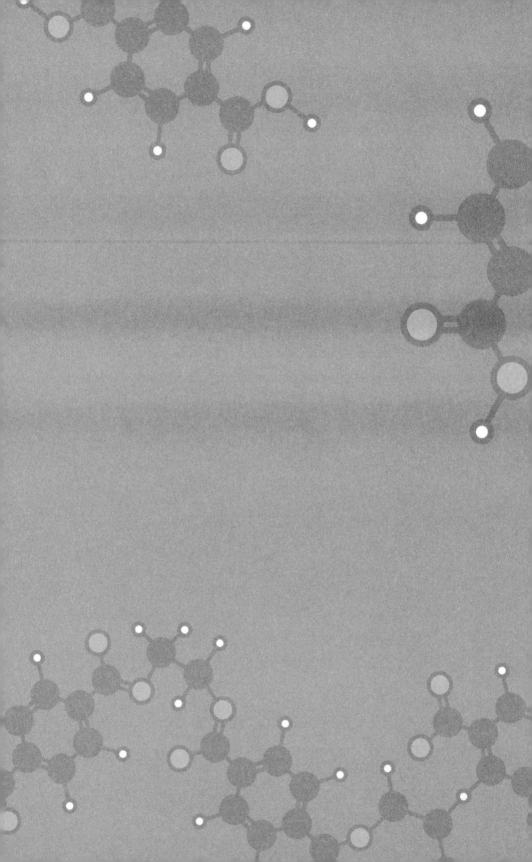

COMPOUND ONE

Know Where You're Going

Early on, I didn't know what I wanted to be when I grew up. Certainly, I yearned to be "somebody." Life in Puerto Rico was tough, and I went through many difficulties as a child. Through it all, my parents promoted education as the ticket to a better life.

And I believed them. As such, I saw that getting a degree could potentially help me to improve my situation. I wanted to not only move into a more accommodating lifestyle but also provide for my children. Moreover, I longed to help others.

It would take time to develop my passion for the pharmaceutical industry. My views about it changed over time, as I learned more and saw the possibilities for advancements. I instinctively have always evaluated therapeutic drugs and thought about the risks before consuming anything. As I grew older, I became more and more interested in the pharmaceutical industry. I realized that I could be more involved, and that I could participate in the discovery and development of new drug therapies to improve health outcomes.

In the following chapters, I'll portray the different attributes of Poly-Esther that are relevant to this compound. We'll consider my passion and how it developed. We'll also look at my feelings of being trapped, and what it was like to be released to pursue my dreams.

Finally, we'll go through the steps that were needed to pursue my college studies. Through it all, you'll learn that I took my parents' advice to heart, and education did open doors. It was far from easy, but oh-so-worth-it.

CHAPTER ONE
The Passionate

"Who wants to play the role of the mother chicken?" the teacher asked.

My hand shot up. "I will!" I added in case she didn't see me.

The teacher scanned the room. Then she picked a different girl (who happened to be very cute!) to be head chicken in the upcoming performance.

This student, amid the others in our fifth-grade class, probably rose to the top in the teacher's mind. She had all the qualities that made her seem like a perfect fit for the main character (and be popular too!). At the time I instantly thought she was chosen because she was cuter or better dressed than me (our typical reaction when someone is selected over us). She would be the matronly figure to all the other chicks in the play.

Our fifth-grade class was putting together a play for the school. I wanted to be a part of it. Time and again, I was overlooked. The teacher chose others for the remaining roles. I didn't get the part I wanted, and I couldn't get it out of my mind.

This story continues, and indeed has a happy ending. Before we get there, let's unpack this a bit more. I'd like to explore it in terms of leadership. Specifically, we'll look at early longings to be something, or someone, of importance. We'll also tread through the benefits of leaning into these ambitions. Finally, we'll look at how we don't always know exactly what we want to be at a young age. The fundamentals may be there, and somewhat hidden to the average eye. As we grow and develop, others sometimes spot in us qualities that we don't see. Pay attention to those times. They could change the trajectory of your career. They certainly did for me.

Middle of the Pack

When I was born, my parents named me Esther Maria de la Providencia Alegria Alicea. (Try writing that as a kindergartner on a piece of paper! It didn't fit!) Most people called me Esther. My father, Antonio E. Alegria, was a widower with four children when he married my mother, Esther Alicea. Together they had four more children. (Yes, we were basically an army.) I was the first of this second set to arrive.

Eleven months after I entered the world, my mother had another girl. Ten months after that she had a boy. Four years later, the youngest member joined the family.

Of the eight children, I was smack in the middle. I had four older siblings, each of whom was very smart. Below me were three little kids, whom everyone described as "cute." Certainly, they were cuter than me.

We lived in Guaynabo, Puerto Rico, during my early years. We moved frequently, though. I found myself having to adapt to new places again and again. Between the changes and my placement within the family, I didn't find myself in many leadership roles as a child. I was more likely to be lost in the shuffle. The fact that the teacher didn't consider me for the main character in the fifth-grade class play didn't come as a surprise. It was more in line with the pace of my life at the time.

Learning the Lines

I was disheartened when the teacher passed over me and chose someone else to be the lead role in that fifth-grade play. The girl who was to be the head chicken practiced every day to get ready for the big performance. I did too. I learned every single line the mother chicken said. I couldn't help it. There was something inside me that yearned to have that leadership position. Even though I was told "no," I still prepared for the part.

I also told the teacher that I knew all the lines. She still didn't give me a chance to practice with the others. Nevertheless, I continued learning because I was so attracted to the idea. Sometimes the kids who were in the play practiced in front of our class. I watched them perform … and said the lines in my head along with them.

The big day arrived. It was time for our fifth-grade class to put on a show. Parents and other grade levels would come to see the chicken-themed play. We all arrived early, jittery and anxious for the big moment.

Some were more nervous than others. The girl who was to play the part of the mother chicken was beside herself. She had performed well during the practices. Now, the image of being in front of a large audience loomed before her. She couldn't face it. Sieged with stage fright, she started crying and broke down. She couldn't go on. She wouldn't be able to be the mother chicken.

That's when the teacher looked at me. "Esther," she said. "I need you."

I stepped in without hesitation. And I got every single word correct. The show—as they say—went on.

For so long, throughout the practices, I had yearned to have that mother chicken role. Even though I didn't see the future or think I would get a chance, I prepared myself. I also let others know. If the teacher wasn't aware that I knew all the lines, she likely wouldn't have turned to me. But because I'd made her aware, when the opportunity came up, it was me she turned to. And I took the show.

Perhaps the best part of this example isn't the outcome. It may be the fact that I got ready, even when the leadership position seemed unattainable. Have you ever taken similar steps to prepare, even though you didn't have the title in hand? If you're thinking of putting in the extra time for a project that someone else is leading, I can assure you that it will pay off in some way—even if you aren't sure exactly how it will look in the end.

Repeat Performances

In Puerto Rico, sixth grade is the final year of elementary school. As such, when I was in that level, much of the year was spent preparing for the graduation ceremony. It would be a big deal. Parents would come. It would signal the end of an era, and the beginning of a new one.

For the celebration, one student in the class would deliver a poem the teacher chose to the audience. This meant the individual who was chosen would need to memorize the lines of the poem. It was a lengthy, elaborate speech, written for adults. It included precise gestures at certain moments for emphasis. It was an important role, and many of us hoped to have the chance to recite the poem.

Of course, I didn't just want to say the poem. I *really* wanted to be the one on stage, giving a beautiful delivery to the audience. Again, when the teacher searched for the right student, I volunteered to do it. Again, she passed over me. This time, she again chose another girl instead of me.

I was devastated at first. Then I looked at the lines of the poem. And I started memorizing. I learned the entire poem, from start to finish. I mentioned to my teacher (on more than one occasion!) that I knew the lines. I could do it, if she needed me.

As it turned out, two days before the big day of graduation, a crisis arose. The teacher discovered that the student she had chosen to recite the poem didn't know her lines! Moreover, her situation was a bit hopeless. The poor girl simply couldn't get the words across. Given the poem's length, there was no way she could learn it in just two days. What was the teacher to do?

As before, I was asked to step in. The teacher knew that I had learned it all. The day of the big performance, I stood up and delivered the poem, line by line, to those in attendance. And I got every word right. Again.

For the record, a similar scenario played out just two years later. I was part of a baton club that was going to perform in a show. It was time to choose the leader. Oh, how I wanted to be selected. I knew I could direct the others in the routine. Sure enough, another girl was chosen. Still, I learned every step.

Two days before our big performance, the parents of the lead girl pulled her out. I was asked to be in the lead position. I accepted, and guided the other participants through the routine, start to finish.

Finding a Place

Given my track record, when I signed up for Girl Scouts, I didn't expect much in the way of leadership roles. I decided to not ask if the subject came up. I simply got to work, learned the tasks, and carried on as I knew best. Pretty soon, I had a strong handle on the activities we did. I helped other girls if they had a question or couldn't finish a task.

This time, when the director of the Girl Scouts announced it was time to pick the Girl Scout leader, I kept quiet. I waited to see who would be picked.

"Esther, I want you to be the leader," the director said.

I looked up. Had I heard correctly?

Seeing my reaction, she added, "You have mastered the activities we are doing. You're not afraid to take the lead. We've been watching you and think you are the right fit for the role."

Wow, had the tables turned! Suddenly someone else was seeing something in me that made them think I was fit for leadership. I never forgot that moment.

At the time, I didn't know in what way I would be a leader when I grew up. I wasn't sure what profession I would take. Certainly, a passion had been born in me to be *something*! What that would be wasn't obvious. It would play out over time. My passion would eventually grow and find its direction.

Listening to Find Your Passion

I once had a teacher tell me, "Esther, you're really smart ... you could do anything."

At the time, I didn't believe it. I had older siblings who were incredibly intelligent. When you live with people who are excelling in their studies, it's easy to consider yourself as less knowledgeable.

That statement, along with the director choosing me to be Girl Scout leader, stayed with me. These messages fanned the small flame inside me. I could feel it burning. This passion would help me later, when I had discovered what I wanted to do for a career. It would drive me to sort through obstacles—even those that seemed impossible to overcome.

I've never forgotten these moments. I'm glad they occurred. I didn't get chosen right away in many instances, but I'm glad for that, because I had to look for what I could do. In these cases, I was able to learn and master certain skills. I engaged, even when the outcome wasn't certain. That way, when the opportunity arose, I was ready to step in—and lead.

Now, after being a CEO and chief innovation officer of my own company, with a PhD and many years of experience in my field, I draw on those early leadership experiences. When I mentor others, I look for areas that they might not see. I call attention to traits that could serve them in their own leadership journeys. If you've ever had a person in authority tell you something praiseworthy that surprised you, it may be a sign to evaluate your strengths. There could be a trait that others are seeing—and you could too.

I remember I once had a mentee who was interested in science and technology, and she was intrigued with improving conditions. I watched her in a couple of meetings. She could take complex problems and think them through. She demonstrated strong potential for further development.

I was a manager at the time. I called her into my office and asked, "What are your aspirations?"

She didn't know. As I spoke with her, I realized she was very humble and had low self-esteem.

I told her, "In those meetings, do you know what I saw? I saw a person who can take a very complex scientific challenge and think it through to find a solution. Not everybody can do that. We need people like you in leadership roles so that we can guide people who are doing the studies."

By the end of our meeting, I got her thinking about moving up. I suggested she be put in a leadership role in a later project. She was very nervous about it. She said she couldn't do it.

I replied, "Why not? It won't hurt you. At the very least, you'll learn something. No one can take that away from you." I made sure the arrangement was a safe environment for her. If it didn't go well, she would simply continue on as before.

Instead, the project had great results. My mentoring helped her to gain confidence. Later I promoted her to a higher position. She became a director. Today she is a senior vice president of a company in Boston.

All thanks to a conversation. And a passion that allowed itself to be kindled, to grow, and to burn bright.

Questions for Reflection

- Have you had moments when you aren't sure if you can be a leader? How did you feel at that time?
- Has anyone talked to you about leadership? What did they say?
- Do you know what your passion is? If not, what drives you? What are areas that interest you?
- Are you in a situation where you could take on more responsibility that goes above and beyond your current tasks?
- What is one step you can take toward finding and fulfilling your passion?

CHAPTER TWO
The Caged Bird

"Esther, did you take your Valium like the doctor said you should?" my grandmother asked. I was seventeen years old at the time, and my grandmother was helping my recently divorced mother manage her household of kids in Puerto Rico.

"Yes," I replied.

But it wasn't true. I hadn't really taken the medicine. At the time, I had been suffering from severe chest pains. The discomfort level was so extreme that I thought I was having a heart attack. It came on suddenly: I had been watching TV (a far cry from anything physically strenuous!) when I felt like I was going to faint. The pain was so great that it seemed like waves of electricity were pulsing throughout my body. My chest was so tight I could barely gasp for air.

In response, my grandmother had rushed me to see a doctor. After examining me, the physician told us that my heart was fine; however, I had signs of a nerve attack. To get my anxiety under control, the recommendation was to take Valium.

In my head, I thought, *What? Take drugs? Isn't Valium wrong?*

In the doctor's defense, knowledge of medicine wasn't as widespread in those days. Specifically, anxiety was just about never talked about. In my case, the doctor was drawing on his background to try to help. While the medication was known to soothe high levels of stress, I was only a teenager at the time. My middle school ran a program that taught kids about the dangers of narcotics and overdosing. They did a good job in their instruction! I had never taken any illegal drugs and I worried that the prescribed medicine, although legal, would be too much for my body to handle or could expose me to other health risks.

Moreover, I had heard adults talking about Valium, and being addicted to it. I questioned the idea of prescribing it to someone so young. Already then, I was weighing the risk and benefits of medications. In my mind, I did a pros and cons analysis of Valium based on what I knew.

I stood by while my grandmother purchased the Valium. I accepted the medicine and pretended to take it. Inside, however, I just couldn't bring myself to swallow it. I remained skeptical and questioned the treatment plan. It appeared odd to me, to a certain extent, that a tranquilizer was prescribed for my condition. I wondered if I needed something more.

I think deep within I knew I was dealing with a bigger issue. That problem couldn't be solved in the same way that you slap a Band-Aid on a cut on your arm or put a pacifier in a baby's mouth to stop the crying. My personal situation involved deep family and emotional challenges, and they were impacting my health. Still, in the end, I never took a single pill.

Before you congratulate me for not using drugs, let me reiterate that it was a dark time in my life, and when I reflect on it, I still have mixed feelings about where I was living and what I was doing. If you grew up in a low-income area or without built-in educational opportunities (or really, any struggle, and I know we all have them to some degree!) and still want to attain success, this chapter is meant for you.

Certainly, my family matters played a role in my mental health during my teenage years (remember, I'm one of eight children!).

Those anxieties from my childhood, which stemmed from experiences including abuse and a divorce, would resurface in different ways later in life, after I was married and looking to pursue higher levels of education. I think it's important to share these here, as I believe my own story can help others see possibilities in their life—even when the horizon looks bleak. As you read the following sections, I encourage you to reflect on your own background.

Searching for Something

When I was growing up in Puerto Rico, my parents divorced, as I mentioned. After the split, I lived with my mother, who kept moving here and there. We spent time on the outskirts of San Juan, the capital and most populated city on the island. From age five to fifteen, I lived in Bayamon, a southern suburb of San Juan that is famous for its chicharron, fried pig skin (you must try it!). I moved to Vega Baja with my mother and younger siblings when I was fifteen and stayed there until I was twenty-four. Vega Baja is home to some of the most beautiful beaches that captivate tourists year after year. They flock to Puerto Rico to relax and soak in what they consider to be a tropical paradise. In both locations, we lived in various residences.

Here's the thing, though. When you grow up in an area, you don't always fully recognize and acknowledge its beauty and aura while you are there. Sometimes it takes leaving to realize just how special it was. In my case, a love for warm weather will always stay with me. And this will become more evident in later chapters, when I land in the "tundra"—which is how Boston and Denmark felt! But first let's reminisce on my sunshine-filled days.

Puerto Rico will always be in me, just as it has been instilled in all who are from the island, regardless of whether they stay. There are around 3.2 million people living in Puerto Rico and close to five million Puerto Ricans who reside in the United States.[1] The territory is just 100 miles long and 35 miles wide, with about 270 miles of coastline and nearly three hundred beaches.

Outshining the topography, which is indeed lovely, are the Puerto Rican people. We call ourselves Boricua, which comes from the word Borinquen, the name given to the island by the Taínos. This group of indigenous people inhabited the island for hundreds of years before the Spanish arrived in 1493. We are vibrant, passionate, proud, and full of life (just have a coffee with me and you'll see what I mean!).

I bring this up because I think it's relevant for our discussion to pay homage to the island's beauty and charm, while simultaneously acknowledging that living there doesn't equate to a sense of paradise. If you think back to your childhood years and have mixed feelings about the good and difficult experiences you went through, you may have a sense of what I mean. In my case, it will always have a special place in my heart and be part of who I am. It will also be the place where I went through hard times in my early years.

You'll recall that my family was full of high achievers. My parents knew that they wouldn't be leaving their kids an inheritance and that they couldn't provide financial support for their education. They saw there was a chance to do well through studying and doing well in school. They pushed us to excel, and by the time I was in the middle of my high school years, that seemed to be happening for me (though some of my siblings were considered to be more accomplished and higher achievers).

I attended the same school for the most part from first to tenth grade. The place was located in the city of Bayamon. I was out of the

---

1   "Facts about Puerto Rico," Discover Puerto Rico, accessed April 6, 2023, https://www.discoverpuertorico.com/info/facts-about-puerto-rico.

school twice for brief periods due to family circumstances. Still, for the most part, I did well—by the time I got to tenth grade, I had all A's.

Then my parents got divorced. When that happened, my mother moved in with her mother, who lived in Vega Baja, east of San Juan on the north coast. As a result, my mother pulled me to a new high school in the area. When I started there, I realized right away that everyone already had their groups formed. I struggled to create relationships there, and I felt so alone.

Around that time, I began to sense that something was wrong with my health. Amid the stress of the divorce, the change of schools, and the intense loneliness I experienced, my nerves were a wreck. I was trying to please everyone, and yet I couldn't find a place where I felt settled. I had my first panic attack when I was seventeen years old.

Finding Pharmaceuticals

As time went on, I worked to manage my stress levels and find a way to direct all my energy. That passion I had felt during my early years of school stayed with me. I knew I wanted to be something, and I longed to have a leadership role.

I kept studying in high school, and also started dating and found my first husband. I was young when we started going out—just fifteen years old! He was older than me, and when my mother learned of the relationship, she emphasized that she wanted me to finish high school. She also hoped I would go to college and get a bachelor's degree. I shared her idea of studying further, as I also saw it as a way to get ahead, move up, and help others.

One month after my high school graduation, I got married. Then two months later I started college. It was for a two-year degree, rather than a bachelor's degree, but at least it was something educational in nature. I loved my classes and was on track to be a pharmaceutical technician and work in the booming industry in Puerto Rico. During the 1960s and 1970s, the US government passed a tax code that granted benefits to companies that manufactured medical products and drugs on the island. As a result, the place became a pharmaceutical hub for the United States. Soon the island housed major manufacturers and increased its exports of brand-name medicines.[2]

It was the start of a new phase for me—not just because I was working toward a degree but because in my second semester, I got pregnant with my first child.

While getting ready for my son's birth, I was also in classes and preparing for exams. I kept attending classes until the very end of my pregnancy. My professors were not used to having a very pregnant student in class, so every time I moved, I would get asked, "Are you in labor?" I would reply, "Not yet, I will let you know for sure."

The professors agreed to keep working with me during my absence when the baby arrived and gave me permission to take the tests after he was born, which I told them would only be two weeks. The day came, and by the third semester, I was officially a nineteen-year-old mother. I wanted to keep my word of only being absent for two weeks, but the birth made it extremely difficult to stay on track with college work.

Still, I tried. Until, that is, an event occurred that changed everything. Two weeks post-birth, I returned to college. The first week upon my return was full of due homework and exams. I drove to classes and then came home for five days in a row. I was so sleep deprived and

---

2   Lynne Chandler Garcia and Michael Beverley, "Reinvigorating Puerto Rico's Pharmaceutical Industry: A U.S. Security Imperative," *CENTRO: Journal of the Center for Puerto Rican Studies* 33, no. 2 (Summer 2021), https://go.gale.com/ps/i.do?p=IFME &u=googlescholar&id=GALE|A677656855&v=2.1&it=r&sid=googleScholar&asid=1 32e1b35.

tired that by Friday, I fell asleep at the wheel. The car veered off the road and crashed into a tree. The vehicle was totaled. Miraculously, I did not break any bones but had no feeling in my body from my waist down. I also had a lot of face scratches from the windshield, which had shattered upon impact. Laying in a hospital bed while recovering from the accident, I sent messages to my professors that I would be out two more weeks. I managed to complete the coursework for the semester and graduated top of the class the following semester. Though I managed to graduate, the accident was enough to make me see that studying would be impractical for the long term.

I also didn't have a lot of encouragement from relatives to continue in school, as they saw I had other responsibilities at home. My husband in particular had a different set of beliefs than me, and he preferred that I tend to other duties rather than school.

Some professors saw otherwise. I loved the subjects I was studying, and math and science came easily to me. I remember one of my chemistry instructors noticed how I was participating in the classroom and scoring high on the tests. He asked me, "Are you planning to go for a four-year degree?"

I responded, "No, I'm a mother."

He told me, "Esther, I think you have the capacity to do more."

Again I replied, "No, you see, my siblings are the smart ones."

I didn't pursue the four-year degree at the time. Instead, I finished the two-year associate program and got my first job at a pharmaceutical company. When I started work there, I learned about the therapeutic drug manufacturing process and how much laboratory testing goes into ensuring the quality of the product meets FDA requirements before it leaves the plant.

And I fell in love—with the work! It was fascinating. I could witness drugs being manufactured that my family and neighbors were using. I felt like I was part of a movement that was making a difference. We were producing something that people who are sick or suffering could use to get better. Soon I was dreaming of doing more. I watched leaders walk the halls and wondered what it would take to be in their shoes.

Then I would go home and care for my baby, anxious about how we would possibly be able to pay the bills and get ahead on the island. My husband struggled to get work and bring in an income, and he looked to me to take care of the daily household chores. I couldn't continue to study, even if I knew it would eventually improve my financial situation. I had to focus on a way to get more income in the short term. Money was so tight that my son would ask for milk, and at times all I could give him was Kool-Aid because it was cheaper to buy (today this memory still haunts me and brings me to tears).

Thus, I wrestled with this inner mix of goals and outer reality of responsibilities. I had discovered a love for the pharmaceutical industry and that's where I wanted to be working. I yearned to be involved, leading people, and working as a scientist. I had a life goal in place. And yet, I had married someone who wanted me to be at home. I had to care for my son and try to stretch our resources to sustain our growing family.

The Crash

Imagine a huge fire of passion burning bright (that's me discovering the amazing field of pharmaceuticals!). Now envision it getting smaller…and smaller…and smaller still. Eventually it is about to die out.

This image sets the scene for my next stage in life. My husband lost his job and our income dissolved. I couldn't work anymore, as I had to care for my son. I was surrounded by siblings who were accomplishing life goals and gaining recognition in their respective fields. One of my brothers had a PhD, one was in dental school, and the others were graduating and embarking on their own careers. For my part, by the time I turned twenty-four, I had a five-year-old son and a one-year-old daughter and was struggling financially even to meet basic day-to-day needs. I felt like I was a black sheep in the family.

What were we going to do? Getting an advanced degree and being a leader was still my dream—but it loomed like a mountain before me. How could I possibly reach the top?

I had no idea, but I was driven to find a way. I had to start at the bottom of that mountain and figure out how to get an income for our family so we could have some sort of stability. Once we had that in place, I reasoned that I would be able to take the next step forward (hopefully up!).

I learned through an acquaintance that my husband could join the army. If he went that route, we could move to the United States and find opportunities to improve our financial situation. I spent some time convincing my husband to go, and he eventually agreed. We set out to Fort Bragg in North Carolina, to the army base where he would be employed.

We arrived broke and were counting pennies just to get by. We didn't even have a washing machine amid our meager furnishings. I hardly knew English—I could read a dictionary, but when people talked to me at the store, I couldn't understand a word. We had no family, no connections in the area, and no support group to lean on.

On top of these struggles, my husband and I weren't on the same page regarding what I would do. While I held that goal of studying and having a career, he took more of a *machista* outlook and saw my role as being at home and caring for the kids. I only had that two-year technical degree, yet he wasn't interested in seeing me pursue more education. This weighed heavily on me. It seemed the top of the mountain was growing further away, rather than closer. *Would it disappear forever?* I wondered.

Soon the difficulties of communicating, our dire economic situation, my inability to study, and the daily grind of caring for two little ones in a place that felt foreign compared to Puerto Rico added up. Symptoms that were similar to what I had felt during those early panic attacks on the island began to revisit me. I stopped sleeping and had a hard time functioning during the day. It seemed like I was always in a hole, and I couldn't get out (talk about a long way from the bottom of a mountain! I had gone into a decline and despair reigned). I would look at my kids and think, *They must believe they have a crazy mother. Something is wrong with me.*

Eventually, when I could stand it no longer, I started considering my options for help. I remember looking through a phone book at the yellow pages. I wanted to find a psychiatrist that spoke Spanish. I came across a name and reached out.

I was able to set up an appointment. At the visit, I explained my situation to the psychiatrist. After listening to my story and symptoms, he told me, "I need to put you in the hospital."

The doctor asked my husband to get medicine for me that evening, and to bring me to the facility the following day. However, my husband didn't believe that I was really depressed—he was convinced I was faking it. He refused to get the medicine. I had to wait to get to the hospital to get started with the treatment the next day.

Starting to Climb Out

I was diagnosed with clinical depression and spent a month in the hospital. That gave the doctor time to try out different drugs and see what worked best for me. It also gave him the chance to learn what was going on. I shared some of my dreams and how miserable I felt in my current situation. I felt embarrassed and out of control with my life at the time. It seemed the darkness would never lift.

One day when my husband came to the hospital, the doctor visited with him. I was there, watching the conversation between the two as it played out. The psychiatrist asked my husband, "Do you want a happy wife? A happy mother?"

My husband replied, "Sure, yes."

Then the doctor said, "Then you need to open the cage."

My husband knew I longed to study and that I hadn't gone back to college. At this point in the conversation, he turned to me and said, "Is this about you wanting to go back to college? That's what will make you better?"

I looked at him and said, "I just want to die."

At that point, my husband realized for the first time that I was not faking it. He knew we had gone through many arguments and fights about college. He always questioned whether I wanted to finish college because of my siblings, and he never understood my reasons for it.

Toward the end of the conversation that day in the hospital, the doctor suggested I go to college. My husband relented, recognizing the seriousness of the situation. He agreed reluctantly that I could enroll. The doctor offered me a four-hour release from the hospital, so we went to the closest college where I could apply.

That moment became a turning point in my life. I saw college as my salvation to force my mind out of dark thoughts. Finally, I had something that would help me work toward reaching my long-term goal. I could put all my energy into my courses. This step helped me to start climbing out of that hole of darkness. It gave me a new motivation and inspired me on my journey. I must admit that there were days when, walking through the campus from class to class, I still felt like there was a long way to go to get back to myself.

While it's common in the business world to minimize our struggles, I have shared this story with others whom I have mentored. I find it helpful in the sense that it conveys several important points. First, stages are not always easy! Even if you don't have a golden path laid out before you, complete with a support system to help you along, there are still ways to move along. In addition, hard times can be used to help us redirect our lives. And here's the best part: once we get through them, we can relate to others who are working to get out of their own challenges.

To end on some good news, I loved my time in college. Of course, it wasn't all perfect and I faced severe obstacles. Don't worry, I found ways to get through those too! In the following chapter, we'll continue with this climb that was just beginning after I got out of the cage. No longer trapped with closed doors for college, I could start to see a future again. I could revisit that dream and focus on reaching the peak. And that's just what I did.

Questions for Reflection

- Have you ever felt trapped in life? What sort of cage have you faced?
- What did it take to get out of the cage?

- Are there current challenges you are facing that you see as limiting?
- What strategies might you use to overcome these obstacles?
- Are there individuals in your life who have helped you to get through tough times? How did you find them?
- How have you resolved periods of loneliness, or what tools could you use to reduce current feelings of loneliness?

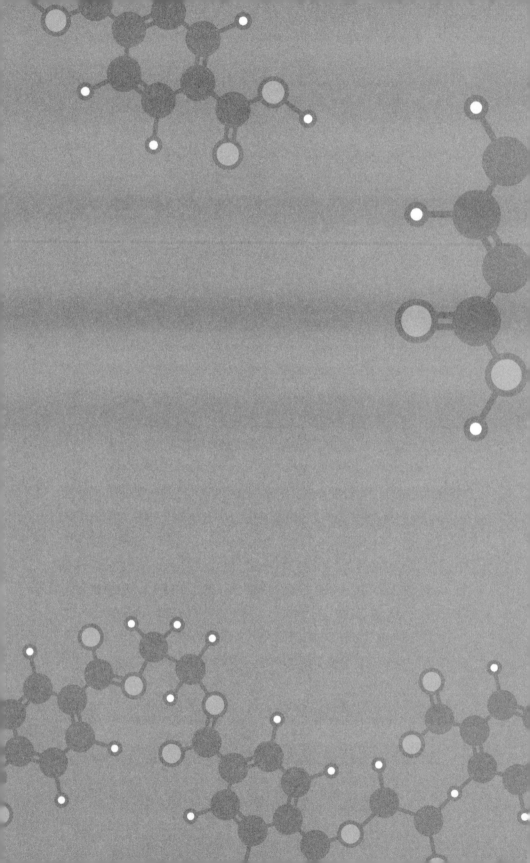

CHAPTER THREE
The Visionary

Do you know anybody that is in the military, or spent time in the military?

If so, you may be familiar with the practice surrounding orders. When commanders issue these, they are expected to be followed. These are often associated with how you'll serve and the base you will be on. If you're new to the military, you can expect orders to come. And when they do, you better be ready and up for anything.

Unless, of course, your name is Esther and you're from Puerto Rico. Oh, and that you discover miracles can happen.

This is my story on how orders can, in fact, be changed (something I have continually been assured never happens! Trust me, there will be lessons in this tale!).

To fully delve into the time the military granted my wish, we must return to my departure from the hospital. We'll need to look at what it was like to start college—with two kids! And how my adapting to English went. We'll go on to discuss the details of how I pleaded to get orders changed ... and then watched the impossible become the possible. Oh, and I got to keep studying to get my degree!

Studying and Rays of Hope

When I went back to college, those initial two years I had put in for my technical degree did not apply toward a four-year program. Others heard about this and told me, "You're starting over." Of course, they were correct in a sense. It would have been wonderful to be able to put those initial two years of higher learning toward an advanced degree. After all, I was in my mid-twenties, my kids were growing, and I was anxious to have a career. Going to college for four whole years for a bachelor's degree appeared to be a long road.

But I would have to take that road to get up the mountain. If I wanted to be a leader in the pharmaceutical industry, I couldn't depend on a mere technical degree. Others might not give me the opportunities for a promotion, and I lacked a strong background in science, math, and chemistry. How could I excel in areas like research and development if I didn't have a foundation to start?

So back I went. I juggled the two kids and classes and dove into the subjects I had to take. I did better with written English than the spoken language during my beginning years. I had studied some English in Puerto Rico. I also took my dictionary with me everywhere so I could look up words.

With each class, assignment, and test, I knew I was advancing toward my goal. I set my priorities and focused on the kids, my homework, and the house. That was it. I didn't have time for anything else. While my fellow classmates were partying or talking or grabbing lunch, I was cramming in my studies and crashing at 9:00 p.m. so that I could be ready to tackle it all again the following day.

A Looming Move

In the middle of those college years, a huge roadblock appeared. It came suddenly, out of nowhere, and was completely unexpected. It had the power to derail me, and I knew it.

It started when my husband got a notice to go overseas. At the time, we were still stationed at the military base in North Carolina. His orders were to go to a military base in Germany.

I was shocked. And worried. Not about life in Europe or what Germany would be like. Rather, my concerns centered around education. I looked and found no colleges near any military base in the country. Remember, this is the 1980s—remote studying and online learning were not a thing yet! Certainly, they were coming and perhaps a form of long-distance correspondence existed in some places, but for the most part, if you wanted to go to college, you had to find a brick-and-mortar building, complete with professors, desks, and chairs.

Up to that point, I had been recovering from being trapped in a cage. My mental health had greatly improved. I credited this progress to the university I was attending. How would a change impact my well-being and studies? Would I ever finish college?

I decided I did not want to find out. Everyone I spoke to assured me that orders could not be changed. Even if they were sympathetic to my case, they explained that it was simply how the army operated. Orders came from the top down and were followed. Period. End of story.

Except, I wasn't finished writing my own story. I did some research and learned that if we moved to Hawaii, we would be on a base that was close to a college where I could continue my program. It would mean saying "no" to Germany and going to the Hawaii base instead.

I asked my husband if he could speak to his commander about our situation. He replied that the orders came from Washington, DC. They were out of the commander's power. He told me it would be impossible to change the decision.

Rather than accept that answer, I thought of a new plan and strategy. I realized that I could talk to the authorities myself. By asking around, I learned the name of the commander who was responsible for those orders to Germany. And I went to his office and knocked.

As I look back on the conversation that followed, I'm certain the commander did not understand what I was saying. That might be because as soon as I saw him, I poured my heart out—and when I'm upset, I talk even faster than my normal fast rate! Plus, with my Spanish-speaking background and my emotions over the looming move, I couldn't help myself and I rattled off everything in whatever language I could at the pace of a high-speed train.

Even though the commander might not have deciphered every single word, my tone was enough. Surely he heard phrases like "No Germany!" I also emphasized, "We need to go to Hawaii." I tried to explain that I would be able to keep studying there. I went into some of the details of my health too. After all, I had done very well in my recuperation plan by attending courses and pursuing my dream of getting a career in the pharmaceutical industry. I hoped the military would support wives who were interested in learning more and advancing too.

In those days, it was very common for military wives to not have opportunities to study and work, due to the frequent moves to any location. There could be potential problems that came from this. For instance, when the husbands retired from the military and settled more permanently in one place, the wives sometimes found themselves in a predicament in which they lacked the skills to get the type of job they wanted. Thus, my situation was an opportunity for the commander to support someone who wanted to carve out a spot too.

After my animated conversation, I left the commander's office. What do you know, a miracle from God occurred next. My husband's orders were changed. We were no longer slated to go to Germany. We were heading to Hawaii.

When he heard the news, my husband shook his head and said, "With you Esther, nothing is impossible." He resigned to going to our new location in Hawaii.

I know this is a miracle, because everyone at the time told me it was! People were dumbstruck and could not believe our change of orders. "No one gets that kind of treatment," they explained. It simply didn't happen (and you'll have to read on to see how I pulled it off again, later!).

The experience taught me a valuable lesson. You have to knock on doors to make things happen. In my case, I figured, *What's the worst that could happen? They tell me "no"? In that case, I'll at least have tried.* The fact is that I did knock on that door, and the door opened.

It would have been easy for me to find excuses to not have that conversation. My English wasn't strong, I had been told that orders couldn't be changed, and I could have given the wrong impression to a superior. Instead, I stood up and knocked. I stated my case. And I got to go to Hawaii.

A Glimpse at a New Vision

Had I simply gone to the military base in the middle of the Pacific Ocean and finished a four-year degree, I may have had an interesting "You won't believe what happened" story to share with others at a party. Let me assure you, my tale doesn't end there! In fact, this small step became one of the many needed to climb the mountain before me.

As I made the ascent, I found an interesting phenomenon occurred. As my exposure to those in leadership positions increased, my goals moved up too. One moment that serves as a solid example of this took place during my undergrad studies. It will forever linger in my mind. It began when a professor reached out to me. I was in his class, studying and loving every minute of it. At that point, I hadn't thought beyond a four-year degree. I saw that achievement as what I needed to really do more in the pharmaceutical industry—at least, at a higher level than the technical degree I had already secured.

This professor called me over and had a conversation with me. "Esther," he said, "You should not only finish a bachelor's degree. You should do a graduate degree too."

I couldn't believe what I was hearing! I started arguing with him. "No, no," I explained, "my brothers could do something like that. Not me."

He insisted, and added, "You should do everything in your power to get that PhD degree."

Well, now I suddenly had a new goal to think about!

That professor was able to see something that I didn't. His encouragement opened my mind and allowed me to consider new possibilities. Getting a doctorate would mean climbing to an even higher peak. My goals were developing, and I was too. My objectives would change as I gained experience. In this case, I was now looking at a steeper summit. It would involve more years of education and a longer wait until I could use my skills professionally.

Still, I couldn't shake his words from my mind. On the contrary, as I looked around me and got to know more about the industry, I grew to realize the value of higher degrees. I would have the skills and experience to potentially take on bigger projects, participate in a greater way toward bettering health outcomes, and get those leadership positions I continued to dream about. I knew that being in a higher position would enable me to be involved in a larger way. I wanted to see the bigger picture and help as many as possible. Thus, I was drawn to leadership roles where I could put those efforts in motion.

This period in my life exemplifies one of the lessons I am always quick to share with those I mentor. As you develop in life and advance on a professional level, your goals are bound to change too. In my case, as I gained more experience and knowledge, I was exposed to new environments. These continued to help me see new opportunities that I didn't think of before. As a result, my goals and vision shifted upward.

While the advanced degree was the new vision at the time, I found later that my goals would change further. You may see this in your own career too. Think about titles like manager, director, vice president, president, and the meaning behind them. If you're in a position below one of these, you may be looking up to get that promotion. Once you have reached a new level, you might start to see what's next. You'll have more interaction with those in leadership too.

We'll further explore these career trajectories in the upcoming chapters. That's because one of my other favorite lessons to share with individuals that I mentor is that getting ahead doesn't always mean moving vertically! Moving up doesn't have to always be a straight-up climb. Lateral shifts could do you well too—as they did for me. For now, let's take the time to unpack this next step I realized I wanted to take. I was up against more years of studying, all the while caring for a household and making it all work financially. It would take determination to get through it—and that's exactly what we'll focus on in the next compound. We're going to look at how to get to your goal. After all, it's one step to set the vision, and it's another to achieve it.

Questions for Reflection

- Are there goals that you are proud to have accomplished? How long did it take to reach them?
- How has achieving objectives in your life impacted you? What changes have you seen in yourself?
- Can you think of others in your life who have helped to open your eyes to new possibilities? What did they allow you to see?
- How have your goals changed over time for your life and career?
- What do you see at the top of your mountain? What are your long-term goals for your life and career?

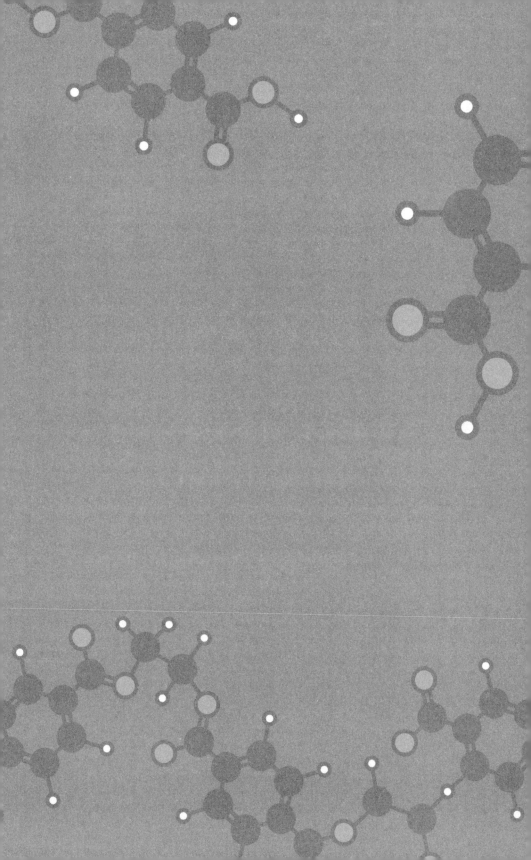

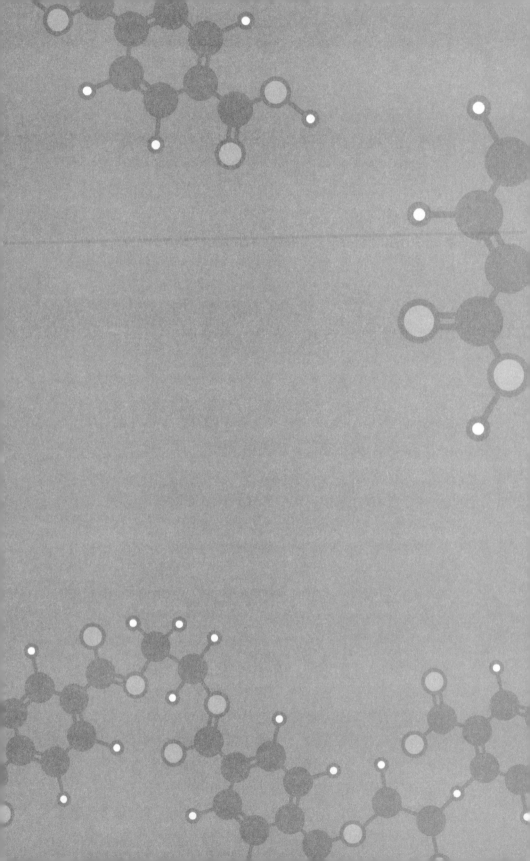

COMPOUND TWO

Different Is Great

I am short, Puerto Rican, and speak with an accent. Oh, and I've lived in different places around the world and worked in an industry dominated by male leadership. So you could say that I know what it's like to feel different!

Beyond that sense of not fitting in, I've come to realize that we, as a society, tend to notice differences. If someone isn't like the rest of us, we might wonder why. And if we are that outcast, it can be easy to hide in a corner. After all, who wants to call more attention to themselves if they are already getting pointed out?

Let me tell you, I have found a new approach to this idea of being different. Time and again in my career, I found ways to use it to my advantage. Rather than cower, I stood up and engaged through my position and role. If I was in a situation where I was the scientist, I sat at the table and represented a scientist—not my accent or looks. When I made mistakes while speaking in English, I laughed about them along with everyone else. Others eventually gave a term to these mixed-up words and phrases: They called them "Estherisms."

As a result, I found that while I will never completely get rid of my accent or grow taller, there is still a place for me. And that place can be at the top. The same is true for you.

In the pages that follow, we'll look at various aspects of "Poly-Esther" that are unique. I'll show how I have learned to embrace them. And guess what? These differences haven't stopped my climb to the top. They have helped me to get creative, to build relationships, and to enjoy the attributes that I can bring to the table. I want the same for you too.

CHAPTER FOUR
The Foreigner

Guess what I did the day after I arrived in Hawaii?

If you answered, "Go to the university," you are correct!

I wanted to check the status of my admission. I had applied to the college but had not yet received an admission letter stating that I had been accepted into the program.

I took my kids along and found a desk where I could ask for help. "I applied six months ago," I explained. I went on to add that I hadn't yet received any word from the university regarding my application.

The people working at the university office that day looked up my case. When they found my folder, they shook their heads. "Oh, you can't be admitted here," they lamented. "English is not your first language. You need to have completed the TOEFL test prior to admission."

How do you think the rest of this episode went? For now, let's just say I wasn't ready to be told "no" and have a door close after pleading with a military commander to move my family to Hawaii so that my mental health could continue to improve and I could remain enrolled in college.

We'll get into the details soon. But I want to pause here and survey this scene. Doing so can aid our discussion for this compound, which focuses on differences. Specifically, I want to talk about how you can use your unique traits to your advantage.

So often, it can be easy to see how we are not the same as others and equate it with a sense of being underprivileged. Maybe we haven't had the same financial resources that others have been able to access. Perhaps we don't have sponsors that offer direction and present career paths to us.

Based on my own background, I'll be the first to say that being different can be a good thing. At the very least, we don't have to see it as a detrimental, debilitating aspect of our lives. In certain moments of my life, I have found that these traits have caused me to work harder and fight more than I thought possible. Rather than backing down or using them as excuses, I discovered ways to turn them into something positive, funny, or meaningful for myself and others around me.

While our exact experiences in life can vary, the lessons are universal. As you read the following sections, think about your own uniqueness. What traits do you have that make you memorable? How could you put a positive spin on certain features you're likely to hide behind? It is my sincere desire that my story will inspire you to remember that your own trajectory can be determined by using your character traits to make the most of your situation.

It would have been easier for me to just head to the beach and forget about pursuing my degree. (Well, maybe so if I had been someone else! But I am Esther, passionate and driven, and I couldn't change that.) My English had greatly improved during the time I spent in North Carolina. However, as you'll soon see, it was far from perfect. And that could have been a differentiator that turned into a barrier too.

No Test, No Semester?

Let's return to that moment in which I'm at the university office, inquiring about my application status. Remember, I have just flown in from North Carolina literally the day before. I'm pulling along two kids as I work my way through the hallways. I need to start studying in Hawaii (since I promised that commander I would if he changed the orders!), and this place is supposed to be my ticket to make that happen.

But because of my status as a non-native English speaker, they didn't want to admit me until I had taken a test, called the TOEFL exam, and passed at a level high enough to qualify me to receive college courses. They looked at the schedule and told me that if I passed, I could get into the university for the following semester.

I was irate. "No one told me I had to take this test," I protested. "If I had known, I could have already lined it up and completed it."

As it was, if I accepted their terms, I would miss a semester. When others heard of my situation, they weren't that disappointed. I remember my mother in particular saying, "Esther, what is it to lose a semester?"

To me it was a big deal. "I don't have the time to move even one semester," I responded. I wrote a letter to the dean of admissions and explained my situation. I shared my story, including the fact that I had been studying at a university in North Carolina that was English speaking. I was surprised to see the requirement, as I had already been involved in a program and thought I was merely transferring to a different place to continue my trajectory.

The dean of admissions called me and asked me to come in for an appointment. I was very nervous. *What if I screw up with my English?* I worried. Still, I went to see him.

When I arrived, he told me that he had read my letter and saw that I was concerned about missing out on a semester of classes. He took out my transcript and looked it over. I had all A's and B's from the previous university. He made a phone call while I sat and waited. When he hung up, he told me that I would be admitted right away. I wouldn't have to lose a semester. I could take the TOEFL test later, after the semester's start, and if I passed, I would be able to continue. "If you flunk it, none of this semester will count," he warned.

I acknowledged his warning and thanked him for his time. I knew I would work hard and pass the test. I would also be committed to my other studies, even though it wouldn't be easy. Our house was located an hour and fifteen minutes, by car, away from the college. I had to drive there and back every day, as I didn't live on campus. I didn't know anyone else that made that kind of commute. But I was determined to make it work and take advantage of the time I had just been granted. I didn't want to lose the semester and I wouldn't let it happen.

Putting in the Hours

Here's some good news: I passed the TOEFL exam. As it worked out with the timing, however, another challenge loomed before me. Since I wasn't accepted with plenty of time before starting my studies, I had missed the cutoff date to apply for financial aid. I couldn't apply for scholarships either. If I wanted to get in and start, I would have to pay the tuition.

But how? Our financial situation wasn't much improved. I didn't have piles of savings to draw on. I couldn't ask my family for help. I knew I needed a loan, or some sort of temporary support, to get me through. In asking around, I learned that I could technically still apply for financial aid, but it would take longer to receive the funds.

My husband looked to his circles for some assistance. When he told my story to others, they were eager to pitch in. Everyone gave a little, and collectively it was enough to cover my initial costs. I kept track of all the loans. When the funds from financial aid came through, I paid everyone back.

Will the challenges ever stop? I wondered. I had put in so much effort to get to where I was. And the truth was, with every new challenge, I felt incredibly alone and isolated to a certain extent. My relatives all lived far away. When I arrived in new places, I didn't have a ready-made support network to catch me and make sure I landed on my feet. But I figured out how to get through each barrier. Many times, it meant asking—and asking again, and again, and again. I found that if I did that, I would eventually find someone who said "yes."

Now I encourage others to do the same. If you find yourself without a circle to help, or if you are in a circle that doesn't have anyone who can support you, go look to see who will. It could be a nonprofit in your neighborhood. Many organizations in communities exist to help the people who are there, especially those in need. I have found that people who have gone through hard times and come out of them are typically ready and eager to pay it forward. If they see that someone could use a hand or some resources, they'll be among the first to extend an offer.

Getting Mad and Laughing

Here's another trick you can use to get the help you need, even if you feel different from others who are going down the same career path as you. You can get angry. While I certainly don't mean you should become destructive, I have found that channeling those high emotions can lead to positive results.

In my case—before you get concerned about my anger management—let me back up and set the stage. In some ways, Hawaii was a wonderful fit for me. I was surrounded by others who were from different places and countries. English was often their second language too. As such, there were many different accents and pronunciations. With so many different backgrounds coming together at the university, there was a sense of comradery among the students. I enjoyed and appreciated this.

Some of the professors were hard on students, and I definitely stood out in class. Beyond being from Puerto Rico and still working to perfect my English, I was also primarily in groups that were male dominated. In one class, called Advanced Quantum Chemistry, I asked the professor a question, and the response I got was: "That is the stupidest question I have ever heard."

That answer made me angry, and it drove me like you wouldn't believe. Not to retaliate, but to work harder than ever. I never wanted to hear that type of criticism again—if I could avoid it, I would. So I studied more than I thought possible for that subject. Due to my extra efforts, I rose to the top of the class. The professor only gave two A's that semester, and I got one of them (that's how mad I had been about his comment to me!).

Situations like this helped me recognize that it's OK to be upset. Use that emotion as a fuel to push you to a better place. In my case, the method helped me get ahead of others in the class. Everything that I saw get written on the blackboard I copied into my notebook. At home, I would look at the textbook, my notes, the course curriculum, and the dictionary. Collectively, these tools enabled me to understand what was being taught in the class. I learned an incredible amount too. And to top it off, I didn't get more ridicule from that professor!

For the most part, I took a different approach when I faced awkward settings. At the university, I took a swimming class because I needed another credit and I figured it would be easier than some of the language-heavy courses. Once inside the pool, I quickly realized I was unfamiliar with all the terms related to swimming. In college I often experienced confusion around communication, and the swimming class I took was no exception. I would look around and follow the lead of others to get by.

The instructor stood at the edge of the water and gave directions to the group for each class. I watched everyone and then did the same thing. I was always about twenty seconds behind! And it was literally a case of "monkey see, monkey do."

Once when I was out of the pool, the instructor approached me. He held his hand to his ear, implying that I couldn't hear. "Are you deaf?" he asked.

It took a little bit for me to understand what he was saying. Once I grasped the question, I laughed. "No, no," I assured him. "I no speak English."

From then on, he was aware of my language barriers. Still, I completed the course by watching others and following along. Looking back, I can't help but laugh at the situation. It was the perfect antidote to get through the communication barriers between myself and the professor.

Moving On—Or Not

Three years into our time in Hawaii, my education faced yet another critical moment. My husband got orders to move to Texas. *What?!* I thought. *I cannot leave Hawaii! I just completed my first year of the PhD program!* I knew it would be best to stay and finish my program there.

I told this to everyone I could, too. Like the previous time in North Carolina, when the orders came to go to Germany, everyone told me I had no voice in the matter. Orders were orders and they didn't change. It would be in my best interest, others urged, to accept it and go.

Of course, I didn't stay quiet (and by now, you are probably not surprised to read this about me!). Again, I pleaded my case to those in authority. I explained that there were so many wives of enlisted military members who couldn't study and have a career. They didn't develop skills that could be used in the outside world.

I told the commander in charge that I wanted to be an example to other women. Here I was, in Hawaii, studying and putting in the hours to be a professional. Perhaps others could see my situation and be inspired to do the same. I begged to stay in Hawaii and finish my degree work.

Guess what? The orders to move to Texas changed. Instead, we were able to stay in Hawaii. This time, when others gasped at the news that the impossible had just happened, I simply put my head down, drove to the campus, and kept on studying.

Questions for Reflection

- What traits do you have that you consider to be unique?
- Have you faced obstacles due to your distinct features and characteristics? If so, how did you get through these?
- Do you see opportunities to use your character traits to your advantage?

- What are some strategies you could use to help you cope with awkward situations?
- Have you ever tried using your anger as motivation to work harder? What about laughter as a remedy to an awkward situation?

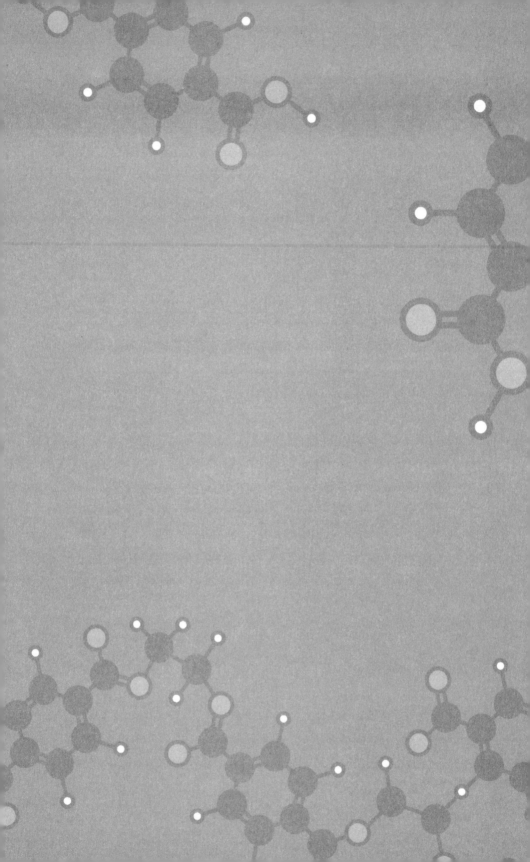

CHAPTER FIVE
The Chemist

Deciding to do a graduate program and get a PhD was an exciting time, but it also meant I was marking myself for more years of school. In addition, I would face challenges at every turn. With my passion, energy, and drive, I thought I was prepared for both.

So I applied for graduate school. And I was told I would not make a great candidate.

Why? I wondered.

At the time, I was still in Hawaii. I had completed my four-year undergraduate work. The next step would be to do the graduate studies. I figured it wouldn't be too difficult to get into the next step, since I had already put in time at the university in Hawaii.

I was wrong. The chair of the Chemistry Department set up a meeting to discuss my application. When I arrived, he told me I was unfit for the program. "Graduate school is not designed for mothers," he said. (Similar to those who told me a four-year degree was not for mothers!)

Well, he obviously didn't know me very well!

His words marked another obstacle on my ascent up the mountain. By this point, my determination was at an all-time high. I had found the medicine I needed to keep my mental health in good shape. It consisted of hard work, studying, and scheduling my kids' activities. I knew I could push through this barrier too.

And I did. In the following sections, we'll go through the steps I did to get through graduate school. As you read, I invite you to think about your own education. Have you had steady opportunities to learn and pursue your interests? Did you find a degree that aligns with your passion? What stood or stands in your way?

Facing obstacles is never easy, but that doesn't make it impossible. Often finding a strategy that works for you, regardless of whether other people are using it, is a great starting point. You can also mentally prepare for one day at a time. For each obstacle that you overcome, you'll grow in confidence. You'll be better equipped to face the next one too.

Setting a System

The professor had a point. Though I didn't agree with him, he was correct that graduate courses required a lot of work. I knew I would have to be highly organized to get through. The program included extensive lab work, and that certainly called for ongoing time and attention. I would have to carry out my research while staying on top of everything else in my life. I pushed to get into grad school, and once I landed in the program, I got to work.

To manage my time, I set a rigid schedule. I would arrive on the university campus at 7:30 a.m. I would go straight to work on my research and other tasks. I would bring my own lunch and stay until 4:30 or 5:00 p.m. Then I would go home for the evening. With this arrangement, I didn't have to go in on the weekends or at nights. I knew I had to be at home during those hours. My husband still looked to me to take care of the house. Plus, my growing kids needed me to help with homework, take them to sports and activities, and attend to their social calendar.

Good thing I fought that professor! Perhaps he believed that because 90 percent of the students around me were single and younger than I was, I couldn't accomplish the same tasks. However, I saw that if I prioritized my time, I could get by. I watched as others took long, lingering lunches. They would usually then stay late into the evening. Some classmates didn't come in much during the day. They had to spend their weekends carrying out research, though. When I got invited to happy hours, I turned down the invitations. I had to be at home, being a mother during those times. I was satisfied with this decision, as it was important to me to be there for my kids. They were the light of my eyes, my inspiration, and they helped me get through the tough periods.

Still, it wasn't easy. My husband often picked fights with me, especially when I was studying. I would have books open all over the dining room table as I studied for an exam. He would walk in and wonder why I wasn't getting dinner for everyone. We weren't on the same page, and in the end, I tried to talk as little as possible about the university when I was at home. He just couldn't accept certain things.

Facing Ridicule

Besides carrying out research in graduate school, I was asked, along with the other students in my group, to present our work periodically. A set of advisors would review it and ask questions. The idea was that they would offer guidance for our projects. They also held the keys to determining if you were doing a good job and worthy of getting that final title, PhD.

For my first presentation, I prepared in a way that made me think I was ready. I had my advisory group selected, and they came to listen to the update I was supposed to share. The event took place in the chemistry building on the campus, which was located right next to the physics building.

I gave my presentation … and the advisors started their attack. Their questions were so fierce and so personal that I had to muster all my strength to get through it. Somehow I gave responses without breaking into tears. When it finally ended, I ran as fast as I could to the physics building. Once inside, I dove into the nearest bathroom.

Others who observed the scene in the bathroom were concerned about me. "What happened?" they wanted to know. I told them that I had just faced the toughest presentation from my PhD board. It took a long time for me to calm down from that episode.

Later one of the professors who had been at the presentation called me into his office. "That was one of the toughest presentations I have ever seen," he began.

Thinking he would offer me sympathy, I waited and listened. Instead of his condolences, though, he started reflecting on his own past. "For the first time I understand my wife," he said.

Now I was slightly confused! But he continued, "My wife and I were in the PhD program together. She downgraded her aspirations to a master's and left because of the tension and what she felt around her. Now, I finally think I understand what she was facing."

His statements affirmed my thoughts that the presentation was brutal. But I knew I didn't want to drop out or shift down to a masters. I wanted to remain strong, and I wanted to finish the PhD program.

Rising Above

I had to keep meeting with that advisory board throughout my PhD studies. My research was directed primarily by one advisor. In addition, there were five people that got together periodically to evaluate my research. The idea was that I would show them my work and tell them what I thought was still missing. They would ask questions and share feedback. (At least, that is how it was supposed to go! My presentations were always tense, and the advisors consistently looked for holes in my research.)

Rather than backing down, their tough stance made me feel angry, and I used that energy to push through. This showed in my other courses too. I competed so hard during graduate school to get A's and a GPA that exceeded 3.5. After two years in the program, any student who had a lower GPA had to take a verbal test. I was excused because of my long list of solid A's. Many of my classmates, on the other hand, were required to do the exam. Their grades were lower, and they managed their time differently than me.

By the end of the program, it was time to present my dissertation. It would be based on the research I had carried out, and the presentation tended to be more of a formality. The advisory group had already seen quite a bit of the work and commented on it. The idea was that they would view your final presentation and then officially approve you for receiving the PhD. (In my case, it was their last chance to grill me one more time!)

I asked if I could bring my children to the final defense of my dissertation. At the time my son was twelve and my daughter was eight years old. Both of them were fluent in English, since they attended school on the island. At home, I always spoke to them in Spanish. It was more comfortable for me, and I wanted them to have an understanding of the language. Because they were bilingual, I knew they would have no trouble at the meeting. They could listen to the English words, and if I needed to tell them something privately, I could revert to Spanish.

The advisory group gave me permission, so I showed up that day all dressed up and with my kids at my side. They sat in the back to observe. At the end, it was customary for the advisory group to ask all audience members to leave. They then asked me their final questions. I made it through that round, and then it was time to go. When I opened the door to leave, I found my two children right on the other side. They had been pressing their ears to the door, trying to hear what was going on inside.

I assured them that it went well. They were so excited and looked at me with big eyes. "Mommy," they said, "I didn't know you could speak English!"

They weren't the only ones surprised at my performance. Remember the professor who told me I shouldn't enter graduate school because I was a mother? He watched me work hard throughout the program. By the end, he had become my biggest fan. When I needed a letter of recommendation for my post-doctoral position at the University of Virginia, he wrote an incredibly glowing report. The person who received it later told me, "This is not a letter of recommendation—it is a letter from a fan!"

Ultimately, I was able to get that PhD in chemistry, and could continue to build new dreams. I was so happy for the opportunity to be involved in the innovative side of the pharmaceutical industry. I didn't know what was ahead, but I knew how far I had come. And those experiences would serve as the foundation to help me get through the next stage.

Questions for Reflection

- Have you ever had to fight against other trends to make your way? What were those times like? How did others react to your choices?
- Have you faced ridicule that impacted how you felt about your life and career?
- What are some ways you might be able to handle criticism and learn from it?
- What are some steps you can take to set your priorities?
- If you were to review and rework your schedule, what changes would you make?

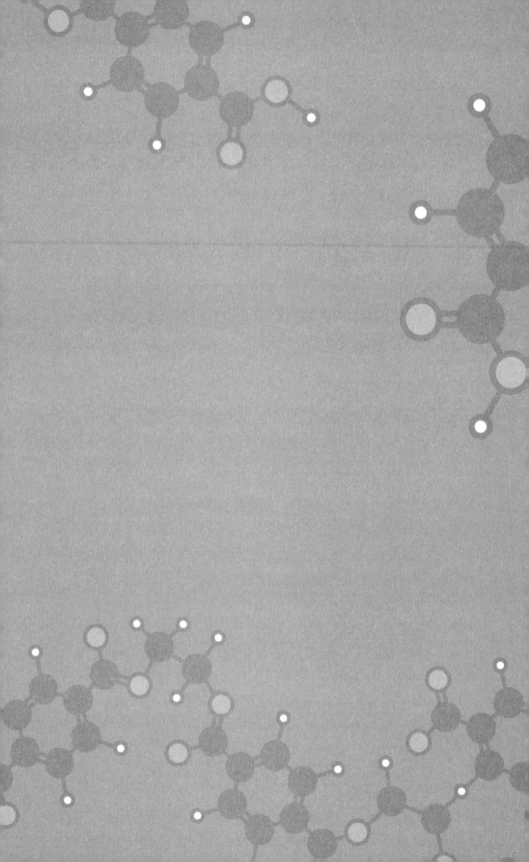

CHAPTER SIX
The One with the Accent

Remember how I mentioned I had to learn English when I got to the United States? I was in my mid-twenties at the time. While I had picked up some basics in Puerto Rico, it took several years and plenty of effort during my college days to become fluent.

By the time I graduated and got my PhD, I was feeling much more confident in my language skills. I could easily communicate with others, and as an extroverted person, I enjoyed the chance to get to know my colleagues. Of course, I carried an accent, as English wasn't my native language.

I never thought much of this, except to laugh about it with peers when I would say something that came across as a little off to them! (Think of words like a "sheet" of paper, and "beach" and how they can be pronounced to get an idea of what I mean!) After finishing college and a PhD program in Hawaii, I moved to Virginia for my post-doc research work and then North Carolina. My career began forming in that region of the mainland. I carried out post-doc work and then took a role as research scientist in a global biopharma developing novel vaccines, which were incredibly exciting steps forward.

Not long into this position—which, let's be honest, seemed like a dream come true after everything I had been through to get there—I started taking on more responsibility. I got a position of leadership and was very grateful for it. Not long after, I went to a meeting with one of the higher-ups. In reviewing my performance, she told me, "Esther, you have so much potential—you are so smart and so creative, you can solve anything that you put your mind to."

These were such kind words to say. I was really touched; after all, I knew how long and difficult the journey to get to this point had been.

Then the kick came. "If you want to grow further in the company," she added, "you have to boot your accent."

What??!!

Let's take some time to look at what happened next. In the following sections, I'll discuss several of the challenges related to language that I have faced. Trust me, there is more to this story than a mention of my accent! We'll look at periods when I worked on speaking clearly, moments when I paused to listen, and sessions when I have encouraged others to use their own voices to be heard.

As you follow my story, I invite you to reflect on your own. Even if you've never had a significant challenge with language or communication, there may be other personality attributes that are so prominent, they could control you. That is, of course, if you let them. Don't worry, as we work to overcome these challenges, I think you'll find that, time and again, the doors to future possibilities are much more likely to open. It all starts by accepting who you are, working to improve where you can, and keeping your eyes open so you don't miss an opportunity when it shows up.

Weeping Over Words

When I was first advised to get rid of my accent, I was shocked. I managed to hold it together until the meeting ended, but then I got out of there. As soon as I was in a private place, I cried and cried and continued crying. I couldn't hold back—it seemed like a door had been slammed in my face. Of course, I had goals to grow and take on more responsibilities. I was determined to create a better life for my children, and I knew that my career could provide that.

I had never before thought my accent would be a hindrance. I wasn't necessarily offended or emotionally hurt by her words—I knew she had good intentions and was trying to help. It was more a feeling of hitting a ceiling that was very hard to bear. How could I rise in my career, and help to improve the lives of patients, if I was stuck on the ground floor due to my pronunciation?

The news was crushing. Though I wasn't a native English speaker, I was definitely fluent and thought I carried myself well. Certainly, I could speak and have in-depth conversations with others. The accent I had when I communicated verbally was simply part of who I am. I spoke quickly, as I always had in Spanish. Those around me learned to understand my pronunciations—and joke with me when the words sounded a little different from what was considered the norm. Besides, I knew many other non-native English speakers who had strong accents.

After reflecting on the conversation, I wasn't sure how I would move forward. So, I did what I always do when I am down—during the days that followed the meeting, I sobbed about it some more. Then I shook myself off and started thinking about what to do. It occurred to me that maybe the company would hire someone to help me work through my "defect." I went back to the person who had told me to get rid of the accent and asked if the company would be willing to cover the costs of a speech therapist. They agreed to the deal.

Here to Stay

Thus began my language escapades with a speech therapist. In reviewing my background, I told her that I had known some English during my early school years. However, it was more "textbook" style, meaning I could read and understand better than I could hear and speak the language. My full immersion into English had begun when I moved to North Carolina at the age of twenty-four.

Here's the thing with languages. If you begin to learn as a child, your mouth and tongue adapt and form to fit the pronunciation needed for certain sounds. When you try to pick it up as an adult, it's a different story! At the start of my speech therapy sessions, I took what was called a test for clarity. I scored 85 percent (not bad really, in my opinion!). With the test, a 100 percent score would mean that I excelled in my pronunciation of words and that I was easy to understand.

I met with the therapist after she had reviewed my exam. At the time, she told me, "Esther, I have bad news for you. The best we can do in these speech therapy sessions is to get you to a 90 percent or a little more … it will never be 100 percent."

She showed me a couple of letters and vowels to help me see where the differences were. For instance, in the case of "v" and "b," in Spanish the pronunciation is the same (Latino readers will be nodding their heads up and down here!). The speech therapist showed me how a word like "ball" requires a certain way of putting the lips for the "b" sound. This is different than the form the mouth takes to say the "V" in "Victor."

I worked on improving the "b" and "v" differentiations in English, along with several others. In the end, I did change the way I said some of the sounds. Though my clarity did increase, the therapist was correct—I never lost my accent.

The speech therapist gave me one other tip that I readily applied to conversations and speeches. She told me to slow down. "Don't talk at the pace that you speak in Spanish," she said. "You won't have time to think about where to position the tongue and mouth, and you'll lose clarity."

I took those words to heart and made an effort to knock down my speed when speaking. If I was asked to give a speech, I would force myself to say fewer words in the amount of time given. I would practice talking at a slower rate and make sure I still fit my presentation within the time frame I was given. I found that the normal rate of speaking is typically about 150 words a minute. Well for me now, it is 115 if I am giving a speech.

After going through the therapy sessions and working on my pronunciation, I met up with an old friend for lunch one day. I hadn't seen her for a year and a half, though we had worked together previously. When we got together, we started catching up on everything. During our conversation, she commented on my accent and the change she noticed in it. According to her, it had improved. Her opinion was a testimony to the speech therapist's work and drove home to me that I had indeed increased my clarity.

Speaking Up

Today, I still carry some of that accent, and I'm glad I have it. People tell me all the time that they love how I talk, and my pronunciation is really a part of who I am. As I reflect on that portion of my life with the speech therapist, I realize that it was helpful to improve the way I formed certain sounds. It's also been beneficial in my professional life to slow down my speech patterns. Whenever I reduce the speed at which I talk, I notice that others can better understand what I say.

Don't worry, there are some words that still make people laugh! (Think about words like "focus"!) As new coworkers and acquaintances enter my life, they often try to correct me at first. They hear the words and phrases I say and point out my mistakes. But as these coworkers and acquaintances become friends, they often refer to these special pronunciations as "Estherisms." They recognize that these phrases are a part of who I am and how I talk. In a way, calling these words "Estherisms" is a term of endearment. We can joke about the distinctions together, and they help identify me as a unique individual.

Now as I mentor others, I always encourage them to speak up, even if it doesn't come naturally. Maybe they don't feel comfortable to share their thoughts, or perhaps they think they don't have anything to add to the conversation. They might, like me, have others making comments about their speech patterns and the risks that these nuances could carry. They may be worried they won't get promoted because of how they talk (or the opposite—how they keep quiet, especially during important meetings when others are looking for their input and feedback).

That's exactly what happened when I moved into a higher leadership position and coached two individuals who reported to me. These guys were super smart but very introverted. I could see they were great workers and deserved to be given more responsibility. But I ran into problems every time I tried to promote them. In order to give them a new role, I had to get the approval of some of my colleagues and superiors. The feedback I received from my peers about those two individuals always differed from my personal thoughts. "They don't talk!" my coworkers would say. "I don't see them as a leader because they are quiet."

Certainly, it is easy to associate leadership with someone who talks a lot. Introverted individuals at times can get passed over, especially if there are others present who speak up more. When people are quiet, it can be hard to know what insight they might be able to offer.

I brought this up to the introverted, intelligent guys I was mentoring (and trying unsuccessfully to promote!). I encouraged them to speak up in meetings. "But I don't want to bring up something that is not new," they responded. They were thinking that if they didn't have anything to contribute, they shouldn't say anything in a group. They would remain quiet until they had a different idea to share.

I could see their point, but the problem was that if they didn't say anything, no one would start to think of them as a leader. I am on the other end of the spectrum! As an extrovert, I have no problem talking to anyone, regardless of my accent! Still, I could empathize with their situation and thought process.

With the goal of helping them, I decided to explain the reasoning behind my urges for them to speak up. "It's not necessarily who brings an idea that matters," I told them. "The important thing is that there is engagement in the conversation. When someone shares a new perspective, you can comment on it. You might say you approve or disapprove of their concept. But when you are in a meeting and you don't engage, it is perceived that you don't have leadership skills. Others don't know if you have strong communication skills or not."

They took in my words and listened to me. I went on to expand my thought to help further motivate them to talk in meetings. "The job of a leader is to make conversations and create paths to progress," I said. "If you are not bringing the idea, that is OK. You can move someone else's idea forward."

Then I added, "If you want to get promoted, you need to speak up—especially when my boss or colleagues are in a meeting!"

Guess what happened next? These two gentlemen didn't get upset with me. Instead, they looked for times to speak up, and fortunately they did this in a way that others could see and observe them! The following year, I tried—again!—to promote them. This time, my suggestions to move them up were well received. They got those promotions. And when the next meetings came, they were ready to participate.

Knowing When to Listen

I mentioned I am extroverted, and talking isn't a problem for me. After I got through the speech therapy, I came across opportunities to move up and take on higher levels of leadership. At one point, after a promotion, I hired an executive coach to help me navigate my new role. I told him, "I know I am so creative and eager to resolve and drive. But sometimes the feedback I get is resentment. Even though I am trying to help, for some people the speed is just too fast. They might want the time to share and discuss, and by rushing forward, I am taking the time away from them."

The executive coach listened to my predicament and then shared this advice. This time, there was no mention of my accent in the conversation! Instead, this coach had a different game plan in mind. As part of his process, he suggested I try active listening. He encouraged me to not talk in meetings. This may have seemed a bit unusual at first, but his aim was to have me soak in what others were saying and how team members communicated to each other. He thought I could learn about communicating and leadership by observing what was going on. I agreed to be quiet during my weekly boss meetings, where all of my colleagues and supporting functions participated.

Well, let me tell you, I sat in those meetings and nearly chewed my tongue off! I had to work so hard to keep my mouth shut for seconds, minutes, an hour, or even more. Trust me when I say it was not easy to refrain from talking.

But I did. And what I learned during those months...wow...talk about life lessons that I still carry with me to this day. The exercise was such an eye-opener in so many ways. As I look back, I can confidently say it was worth it. Did I grow!

For the first time in my career, I was able to study human communication in a new way. I just listened to everybody and observed. Do you know what I saw? First of all, most of the time, in those meetings that I watched, nobody listened to anybody! One person would make a comment, and then another person would talk. What the second participant shared usually had nothing to do with what the first individual had said! Sometimes there was little to no progression on a topic or issue at hand. During other sessions, there wasn't a strong management system to guide the conversation.

These insights helped me reflect on my own styles for guiding a meeting. They made me think about strategies I wanted to implement when I was in charge of a discussion. Some of my conclusions involved guiding the conversation, acknowledging others, and watching body language.

Speaking of body language, one of the biggest takeaways—and surprises—that I gained from that executive coach occurred after he attended one of my meetings. He was asked by human resources to attend a session in which I was participating, along with my peers and boss since he was also conducting a communication workshop within our department. Afterward, he shared his observations with me.

Here is what he said: "In your meeting, I noticed there were two individuals who feel threatened by you." At first this was almost funny to me. Who feels threatened by someone like Esther? I thought my personality was far from intimidating.

He went on, "I could see in their body language that they were hating every word you said. They will not work with you." Interestingly, I had never perceived those individuals as having issues with me. It didn't seem right that they would be worried I would somehow dominate them or take a position of power that they had wanted (like another promotion!).

As I thought about it, the executive coach had given me incredible insight into my working world. Turns out, there were a couple of individuals who were sure that I would get a promotion they were wishing for. In response, they were not at all looking for ways to try to support me. In fact, the opposite was true.

Beyond these points, the coach shared that my superior had certain techniques he used to direct the meeting. "Your boss knows what he wants to hear," the coach said. "He waits to get it. To be a leader, you'll want to learn how those conversations happen. What is the body language that you will bring to the table?" I learned that I didn't necessarily have to talk to run a meeting. I could use a sense of presence, along with gestures and posture, to influence the conversation. After all, my coach pointed out that the majority of the communication happens via nonverbal mannerisms. In today's world of video meetings, nonverbal communication is still key in leadership development. Have you ever noticed what happens if participants keep their camera off? When that occurs, attendees miss more than 90 percent of their communication influence. Have you ever noticed someone who is in a meeting and seems to be reading something else and not engaged? I certainly have. Nonverbal communication in face-to-face meetings and video meetings is still a critical factor for success as you work on further developing your career.

As I look back on these periods of my life, ranging from the speech therapy sessions to when I sat through meetings biting my lips to make sure I was quiet, I think, "Who would have thought that someone who was told to get rid of their accent would encourage others to speak up, and also find it helpful to shut up?" Over time, I learned to manage this balance of engagement. Listening is an essential skill for communication, and expressing ideas in verbal form at the right time is vital as well.

Collectively, these stories drive home a point I am eager to share with those I mentor today: don't let your differences be a hindrance. They don't need to be; they can be indicators of areas where you can improve, but you don't have to fundamentally change yourself to advance in your career. You can learn to listen at the right times, to acknowledge what others are saying, and then share your thoughts to move the conversation forward.

People thoroughly enjoy listening to my non-perfect speech patterns and word choices. When they tell me they adore my accent—I believe them! My accent reminds me how being different can be great. It helps set me apart and enables me to find something to laugh about with others.

As you look at your own life and leadership potential, remember that what is most important is what you can bring to the table. It can be easy to focus on what sets us apart from others and feel intimidated if we think we don't measure up. We might think, "I am too short, too tall, too thin, too big, my looks are different from everyone else, I am the only female on the team…." I am sure you can come up with more. I'm here to say that there's no need to hide in a corner! When you sit at a table you should focus on what you are bringing to the table (the new ideas, solutions to the current challenges…). If you feel you do not have anything to bring, go outside the company and read about other industries, experiences, and challenges to provoke your mind with new thinking. Use those unique traits to your advantage. They are what make you special and can help you stand out in a positive way. They could even give you the chance to lead in a small, medium, or big way, depending on your goals and ambition. When others see that you can contribute in a real, genuine way, those doors that were closed for so long can start to open. As they do, get ready to push a little yourself and step in; then take the opportunity and run with it, laughing along the way.

Questions for Reflection

- Have you ever struggled with communication?
- Do you find it difficult to be heard or to understand others when they are speaking?
- What are some ways you might be able to improve your professional communication skills?
- Are there body language or speech courses available through your employer?
- If you could change one thing about the way you carried yourself, what would it be?
- What speaking traits are you most proud of? Why? How can you use these strengths to your advantage?

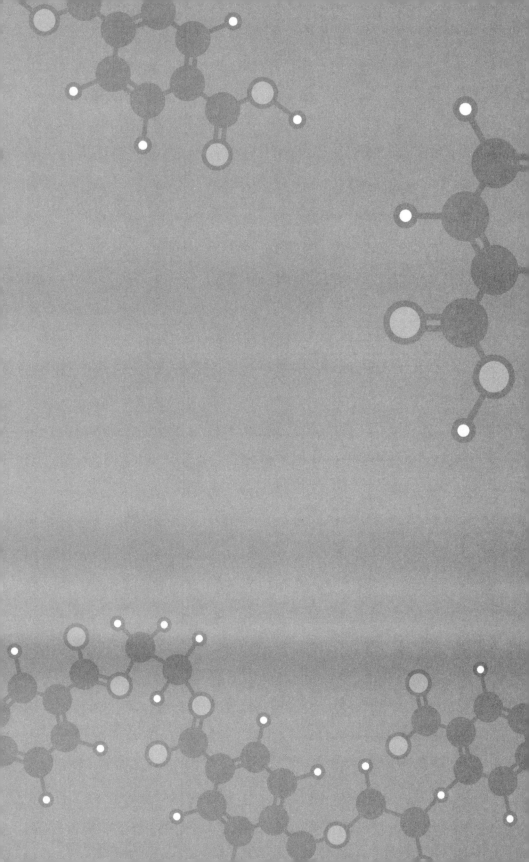

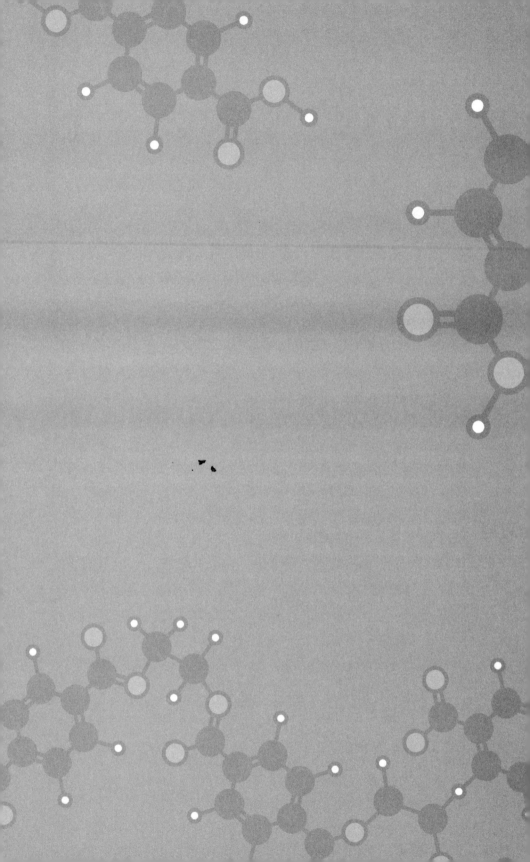

COMPOUND THREE

Keep on Knocking on Doors

When I hear the phrase, "Knock on doors," it causes me to think of so many things. Maybe it does for you too, or perhaps it leads you to think of one of its most common uses. The idea behind it is to keep trying, especially if opportunities don't just appear before you. We often have to seek out the chance to move forward at work and in our career paths.

But for me, knocking on doors goes back to my childhood and early adult life too. I had a rough upbringing in some ways, in terms of family life. I grew up in a household that was separated by divorce, plus I have many siblings and we all have differences among us. Topping that off is the fact that I was raised in a low-income family with few opportunities available.

When I was young, I had to reach out at certain times for help. I did so, calling on people I knew I could count on like my grandmother. I also knocked on doors as a teenager, trying to connect with my father, who was often on the other side of that closed door.

Later in life, as I sought ways to break into my career and build a better life for my children, I continued to look for job-related opportunities. I found that sometimes the answer was an initial "no," and so I had to keep at it. It occasionally got to the point where I wondered if a door would ever move enough to make even a tiny crack for me—and I learned that something always opened up eventually. The key was to put in the effort and not give up.

As I reflect on this compound and the parts of me that it represents, I am thankful that I kept trying. When I was young, and I heard from my parents that education was a ticket to a higher quality of life, I took that to heart. I worked harder than I knew was possible to reach the goals before me. And after reaching one milestone, I found that you have to keep knocking to get to the next. The path isn't always easy, but that feeling of elation when a barrier is broken and you can get through is so worth it.

Come along with me in these next chapters as we find moments to laugh about, shed a tear over, and jump up and down together. I hope seeing these different parts of me and my life will energize you to knock on the doors in your own life. If you don't see an opportunity right away, keep at it! It's a way to build resilience into your Poly-Esther self. The next time you pick up the phone or ask someone to give you a chance, the answer could be "yes."

CHAPTER SEVEN
The Consistent Door Knocker

How many times do you have to be told "no" before you give up? Several times? Twenty or thirty? What about one hundred?

In my case, the correct answer for when to give up would be: never! There have been times when I have made literally hundreds of requests before getting a positive response.

Let's back up a little bit to a point in my life right after getting my PhD. At the time, I was ready to do post-doc work. Do you think getting a degree I had struggled to complete put a bounce in my step?

It most certainly did.

It also meant that I had more work to do.

Specifically, I needed to find a place that would allow me to carry out research and gain experience so that I could branch into the innovation and research and development sectors. I dreamed of pursuing this, but getting a position in those fields would mean reaching out … and reaching out … and reaching out some more.

At the time, when I was in Hawaii and knew my graduation from the doctorate program was approaching, I started looking into the options. I wrote letters to organizations in the United States that I thought might consider me and give me a chance to carry out post-doc research. I explained what I could bring in terms of my credentials, and asked if they were interested. I hoped someone would extend an offer for me.

During this search, I contacted hundreds of places. And I received nearly that many "no's" in response. Who would take me? I started to wonder. When should I stop writing letters?

In the end, I finally received two great opportunities that stated I could carry out my post-doc work at their location. These were Yale University and the University of Virginia. I was so excited I could hardly believe it! The decision went to Virginia as I did not think I could handle the colder weather at Yale, which is located in Connecticut! It would mean a change from the university in Hawaii to Virginia in the United States. I knew it would be worth it and would advance my career, which in turn would be beneficial to my two growing children. Had I given up, and stopped writing letters and pursuing the chance, I wouldn't have received that "yes" and moved forward.

In this chapter, I want to touch on the value of consistently knocking on doors. This trait is far from easy, yet it does typically lead to results. Throughout my life, I've watched what can happen when you keep asking.

In the sections that follow, I'd like to look at an earlier time in my life when I kept knocking on doors. I'll also cover how it has impacted my professional growth and career. It is my hope that the incidents I share will help you as you pursue your own goals. If you ever feel down about carrying on, or if you have fallen down and found it hard to get back up and shake off the dirt, this chapter is for you! Let's dive in.

Family Doors

My family life growing up was pretty hard. My parents had gone through difficult times. In my father's case, he had wanted to become a lawyer in his early days. But he was pulled into the Second World War and was never able to finish his studies or get a career.

At home, with eight kids under tow and some strict policies in place, my father was not an easy person to be around. He didn't allow us to bring our friends home, and he had explosive, violent episodes. He would consistently lock us in the house so that we couldn't leave—literally closing doors on us and keeping them that way.

For many reasons, including the layers of physical and verbal abuse from my father, I begged my mother to get a divorce. She was afraid of him, as he often carried a gun and threatened us, but she felt like she needed to provide her children with a father. At one point when I had just turned fifteen years old, not knowing what to do, but convinced that we had to get away, I called my grandmother. "You want to see us alive?" I asked her. "Then you have to come get us."

My request stemmed from the fact that we couldn't get out of the house. My father had us in his trap, which included a fence which ran through the interior of the home. The system made it possible for us to be securely locked down. I knew we were in danger if we stayed there. Things were not going to get better, no matter how much we wished they would change.

After my phone call, my grandmother and mother started planning an escape. Over time, we packed up our meager possessions and hid them away so it wouldn't look like we were getting ready to move out. Finally, we had everything ready to go, and my grandmother paid for a moving company to come and take away our things quickly.

My parents did get a divorce, and I lived with my mother and grandmother in the countryside. At times, feeling torn by our family troubles, I would take public transportation back to our previous home, where my father still lived. I would knock on the door and wait for him to answer.

When he opened the door and saw it was me, he often replied, "I don't have time for you. You didn't make an appointment to see me."

Then he would close the door in my face.

You can imagine what that series of events, culminating with the door slamming in one's face, does to a person. In my case, it may have triggered some of my early panic attacks and later bouts of depression. At the time when it occurred, I didn't know any different. All I knew was that my friends weren't talking about violent home life, broken families, and pangs of electricity flowing through their body (which is what my first panic attacks felt like). And I also was familiar with what it felt like to get a door slammed in your face.

The Door Knocker

I share these stories—of all those letters I wrote to get a post-doc position, and of my father locking me behind doors or shutting them on me—because I think they serve a purpose for our discussion. Sometimes when we go knocking, we get a positive response. Other times, we're taught lessons to apply in the future.

Throughout my career I have had to remind myself of the power of consistency. If one door doesn't open, it's worth going to the next one. And the one after that. And the next. And so on. It can at times seem endless and overwhelming. I always tell myself that I won't know unless I ask. People and organizations can always say no, but if you just sit there and assume they will give you a negative answer, you're not giving them the chance to open the doors for you and extend an offer.

In the case of my early family life, I suppose one could point out that the case is a bit tragic. It doesn't have a fluffy, packaged result that we often see in business or self-help books. I think it's worth including, though, for several reasons. First, it helped shape and form me. The traits I've developed have stemmed in some way from my early events. For example, I went on to marry a first husband with habits akin to my father. And the weight from the family issues on my shoulders eventually played a role in the development of my anxiety and depression. But those childhood events would help me understand that the road isn't always smooth. We can have hard things happen and still keep our head up.

Fires and Corporate Housing

When we just ask around, there can be positive, pleasant surprises. I have been floored on numerous occasions by the generosity that others have displayed. One case in particular always springs to mind when I think of people who were an incredible gift in my life.

I found my first mentor at a company where I worked early in my career. He was from Taiwan and also spoke with an accent (dare I say he had a stronger accent than me!), and he would go above and beyond for me—even when I wasn't specifically asking him for help. I got to know him over the time I was working at the firm, and he was always so interested in my well-being.

At the time, I was living in a small place with my two children— that I burned down! One Saturday, I left milk heating on the stove and left. Fortunately, nobody was at home when the fire started. As I approached the house when I returned later that day, I noticed something had happened, but I didn't realize until I was nearly there that it was *my* house! The fire department had come and put out the fire, but unfortunately the water used caused so much damage that it wasn't possible to live there anymore.

I had so little money at that time ... I didn't know what to do next. Going to a hotel would be too expensive, and I didn't have any family in the area to take my two kids and myself in. I started asking coworkers if they had room for us to stay while I gained my bearings again.

My mentor must have caught wind of these requests, though I didn't directly ask him for help. Shortly after I burned down the house, HR approached me and said that the company had housing available for myself and my family. Sure enough, my Taiwanese vice president had insisted that I stay in the corporate housing that was available. All I had to do was cover utilities like water and electricity—the rent was covered by the company.

Instances like this serve as an example of how powerful a simple request can be. I have found that many individuals who have achieved some level of success are open to helping out others. But if you don't knock on their door and share your story with them, they won't be aware of how they can help you.

If you're unable to find assistance within your own circles, I encourage you to reach out elsewhere. Head to a nearby church or community center, as these places sometimes have programs that can help. Look for a nonprofit that specializes in professional development and check if you can take a class. Ask at your workplace to see if anyone has a connection in the field that you are interested in. Volunteer at a place that is in your industry as a way to get your foot in the door. While you're there, look for ways to contribute and put in extra time so others can see you are searching for more opportunities.

When you get to the door and are ready to knock (or have drafted an email), you will likely be nervous about the next steps. Take my advice: do it anyway. Open your mouth and ask for help. The nerves will go away, and the people who answer might have been waiting for the chance to help someone like you.

One final thought to keep in mind: Keep your composure at every step. If you reach out to others, maintain a friendly attitude and avoid getting into heated discussions. Having integrity can carry you a long way, regardless of what industry you're in. We'll look at this more in the next chapter, as I point out ways to remain diplomatic in all situations.

Questions for Reflection

- Are there individuals within your own circles who might be able to help you? Have you approached them? Is there anything you could offer them in return for their assistance?
- Do you know of nonprofits in your area that might be able to provide financial aid or mentoring? If not, have you carried out research to find what might be available?
- Is it easy or difficult to ask for help?
- Are there individuals in your life who have helped you in significant ways? If so, is there something you can do to express your gratitude to them?
- Have you thought of ways that you might be able to help others in need? How might that look?

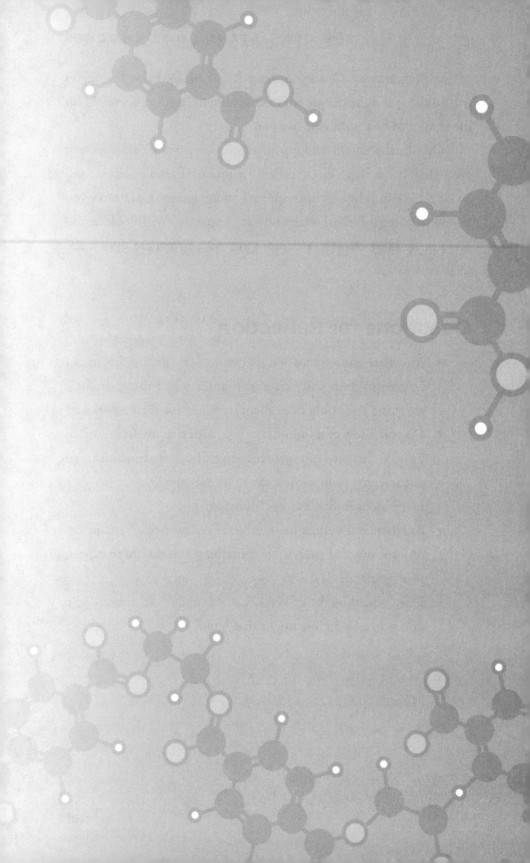

CHAPTER EIGHT
The Ambitious Diplomat

When I was looking around for a job after completing my post-doc work, I applied … and applied … and applied some more. To make things even more challenging it was the fact that I was constrained to North Carolina, if I wanted to take a shot at keeping the family together (my husband at the time was assigned to a North Carolina military base). I couldn't just slide into a perfect job; it took a lot of hard work. At one point, I called an organization that I was interested in, which was a global biopharma doing R&D on new vaccines. When the receptionist answered the phone and I identified myself, she said, "Esther, we know who you are." That's because I had already reached out so many times! (What can I say, it's how I am. Plus, it often works!)

As we talk about the power of persistent asking, I think it can be helpful to take a step back and remember that we always want to present ourselves with integrity. Even in situations in which we feel wronged or passed over, it's vital to act with dignity. I'd like to share a couple of examples in the following sections. As you think about these, I encourage you to evaluate your current professional and personal environments. Ask yourself if there are strategies you can implement to ensure you're treating others with respect and acting in the best interests of everyone involved.

Partnering Up

What's it like to be a woman and go into an industry that is male dominated, especially in the leadership positions? I think you will know what I mean when I say that I have had my moments. Let me share an example with you that might shed light on the type of environment that often surrounded me. It will also outline my strategy of handling it with dignity and moving on.

At one point, I worked at a pharmaceutical company and often participated in meetings with others in positions of authority. I found that nine times out of ten, if I shared an idea, it would get shot down. However, suppose someone else presented my same idea ten minutes later. They might get credit for their great concept. No one would recognize what I said or ask for my thoughts.

Needless to say, I thought there could be a better approach to this. Sometimes I would pull a person aside after the meeting and talk to them about the overlook. This often helped ease tension and occasionally resolved the issue at hand.

For a time, another female leader participated in these meetings. On the side, away from the group discussions, she and I compared notes. We both felt that we were often forgotten in the meetings. We might make a recommendation and have someone tear it down. Or we wouldn't get asked to share our opinion on a matter.

We decided to make a deal to support each other. If, during the meeting, I gave a suggestion that was shot down, we would keep listening. Often the same idea was presented a little later by someone else. Then my colleague would say to the group, "Yes, thank you, and isn't that the exact same thought that Esther shared several minutes ago?" By doing this, we could help each other gain some credibility.

We could also make a subtle point, demonstrating to those at the meeting that we had a voice and expected to be heard.

This strategy worked much better than other possible approaches. We could have raised our voices or caused a heated discussion if we had addressed the issue in a more direct way. Instead, this diplomatic method helped us to be heard. It also kept the atmosphere as calm as possible.

I've continued this strategy in other situations and have found that polite conversation can often get you further than back-and-forth arguments. At times I have pulled coworkers aside after a meeting and talked to them on an individual basis. If I show them respect, they are generally eager and willing to return that attitude. We're able to work out our differences in a diplomatic way—even if the outcome isn't what we hoped for. We'll look at that aspect next.

Dealing with Disappointment

Mira (Look), we all face disappointments. In fact, I think it's fair to say that you can expect to have them all the time (I know I have!). In the professional world, this can take the form of getting passed over for a promotion. You might go and ask your boss for a raise or for a higher position and not get it.

Now, here's my advice for those tough times. You have three choices in those types of situations. You can (1) play the victim, (2) become resentful, or (3) grow determined.

Here's what I say to those stuck in the first approach. When we feel like we are the victim, it is easy to think, "Everybody is against me." You might feel poor or helpless in your situation, and these thoughts can lead to a dead end. It won't be simple to find a solution; in fact, it could seem like nothing will work to make it better.

For the second type of response—resentment—there's also bad news. You might grow to hate everybody that you perceive as an obstacle. These individuals will appear to be against you, even if the scenario is imagined on your part. There could be a misunderstanding or another explanation to the situation. The others involved might not have poor intentions; it could be the result of a lack of communication or misinterpretation of actions.

Remember when I wanted to be the mother chicken in the school play and I was told "no"? Had I chosen to be a victim, I would never have learned the part on my own. If I would have opted for resentment, I would be here today moaning about how I got passed over for another student (*boohoo! Poor me!* You can hear it, can't you?!). Instead, I chose to learn the part anyway. Through sheer determination—though I probably didn't know how to define it at the time—I got to work and knew all the lines. By opting for this approach, when the opportunity arose to fill in for the part, I was ready. In fact, I was able to do more than just get through it. I shined in the role.

I wasn't chosen to perform the speech, but I prepared anyway. Determined to see it through, I was ready to step up when my chance came. The same held true for the role of the baton leader: I practiced instead of moping around and sobbing about it (though I did shed a few tears before my big moment came! My point is that I still worked hard and didn't give up). The pattern has continued throughout my career. I applied for positions, and I was told "no." So I went and cried about it, and then moved on. When defending my research work for my PhD, I could have chosen to be a victim, or resentful. Instead, I opted to do my best … and the rest, of course, is history. I got that PhD, and it's not going away!

Regardless of whether we are looking for ways to deal with disappointment or be heard in some way, there are opportunities to act in a dignified way. I always aim to keep my voice steady, as anger can cause a disagreement to escalate and become unproductive. Also, you'll win more friends along the way if you carry yourself with integrity. Others will notice and be attracted to the model you portray. And later, if you need a helping hand, they'll be happy to extend an offer, enabling you to rise and grow together.

Questions for Reflection

- What are times in your life when you feel you've been passed over?
- What are some ways you'd like to carry yourself with dignity in your professional life?
- How can you be diplomatic in your personal life?
- Are there opportunities to help some of your peers as they work through challenges?
- How might you demonstrate integrity and dignity to others?
- Do you have a role model to follow that consistently acts as a diplomat?

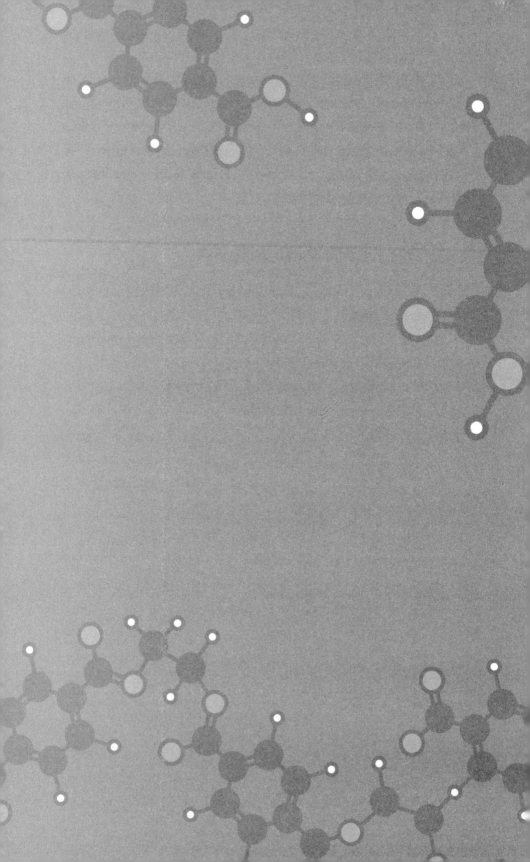

CHAPTER NINE
The Daredevil

What do jumping out of planes and keeping your word have in common?

Allow me to share.

I've gone skydiving three times. And guess what? I hate heights!

In fact, whenever my children—who are now grown adults—ask me about my skydiving attempts, and my reasons for doing what I did, I shrug and jokingly say, "I think I was suicidal."

That said, this type of "suicidal," as it pertains to my skydiving sessions, is a bit of a lighter phrase in my family circles. It can be a great teasing point. I always laugh alongside my children when it is brought up.

It was a foggy time of my life. I was going through something that wasn't humorous at all. You see, early in my professional career, I divorced my first husband. The initial separation occurred shortly after I received my PhD. Really, though, we had drifted apart long before then. After finishing my post-doc studies in Virginia, I shifted back to life close to the military base in North Carolina. My husband at the time felt we had grown apart. Although at the time I would have done anything to keep the family together, we finalized the divorce after eighteen years of marriage.

Needless to say, some incredibly difficult days followed. Those first weeks after the separation turned into months, and collectively remain a bit of a blur in my memory bank. I wasn't in a hospital during this stage, fighting to hang on to my life and find a sense of purpose. However, it was a dark period in terms of stress. The load was great, and some evenings I wondered how I would make it through another day.

In the split, the children remained with me. Between caring for them and coping with the separation after being together for so long caused a great weight to fall on my shoulders. By this time, Jesse and Lili were teenagers, twelve and sixteen years old, going through their own challenges. I barely had the mental capacity to get myself through the day, and the kids were also having a hard time adapting to the change.

So I fell. From a plane. But before we get to that point, let's look at some context. As you absorb the tales that follow, I ask that you think about painful, hard times in your own life. Did you ever feel like your streak of bad days would never end? Have you ever wondered how you would possibly get out of the mess you were in?

While I'm not encouraging you to dwell on those negative memories (or current struggles), I mention them as a connecting point. Those hard times can often help us gain perspective on our lives. Once we get through them, we can look back and remember the silver lining. And we can think about what we will do differently the next time we face such an obstacle.

Now, without further ado, let's talk about skydiving.

Adventuresome and Deathly Terrified

You'll recall that I married very young—I was just eighteen years old. So when I divorced after nearly two decades of marriage, I was merely thirty-six years old. One of the first steps I took after the split was to take back my family's last name.

I wasn't comfortable sharing my personal situation at work—I was pretty new to a company and was still coming to terms with my changing reality and single status. But when people saw that I had changed my last name to "Alegria," they congratulated me. They thought I had gotten married! I had to correct them. "No, I didn't marry someone. I got divorced—I took back my family name." Alegria literally means happiness in English and I definitely give honor to my last name!

"Ohhh," others would reply. It took a little bit for this bit of news to get around. Then, my coworkers started drifting my way. "Have you thought about going out with (fill-in-the-blank)?" they would ask. "What about a blind date?"

During this time, everyone around me suggested to get out more. I did not know what it was like to go out! I started dating the same person I married when I was fifteen years old. So I took advantage of these matchmaking offers. I went on many, many first dates during the following four years. (One day I will write a book on blind dates—watch for it!) One of these outings was with a family doctor, who took me to a place for dinner. Over the meal, he asked, "Esther, do you like adventure?"

"Do I like adventure? Why, adventure is my second name," I replied, full of confidence.

After the date, he called me. "I got two tickets to go skydiving next Saturday," he shared.

I couldn't believe it.

I mentioned earlier my immense fear of heights. I hate flying, to start. One time in my past I was on the 28th floor of a building and the people I was with wanted to show me the balcony. I fell to the floor; I was so freaked out about it.

But what could I say? I had told this guy that I was adventure-some. I couldn't back out.

I decided to go for it. The dive would start at 12,000 feet, and I would be doing a tandem jump with an instructor. I wouldn't have to worry about maneuvering down.

The day of the jump, I was all smiles at the beginning. I put on a fake front and chatted it up with the instructor. I asked about their training and how they would open the parachute. The instructor stated that it was me who should pull the cord to open the parachute. He asked me to count to thirty-five before pulling on the cord to start the parachute. He shared how I should position my legs for the landing and added that I should enjoy the free fall of 8,000 feet! I was working so hard at looking confident that they didn't see how nervous I was.

But I was terribly scared. And those nerves grew. By the time we got in the plane and climbed to 12,000 feet (and it was a tiny plane!), I was ready to lose it. I completely panicked. When it was my turn to jump, they screamed loudly, "Are you ready?!" and I screamed back, "Noooooo!!" They had to push me out the opening. At that point, I forgot how to count to thirty-five and the instructor had to open the parachute himself. I vomited all the way down, and he had to take care of me in the sky. By the time we reached the ground, I was brain dead. I couldn't react or move or do anything.

Next Rounds

Let's take a quick detour here for just a moment so I can share with you that I didn't stay with the family doctor. He wasn't the one for me—though he was indeed full of adventure. (I did, however, go on many blind dates after that and my romance story eventually found a happy ending that we'll get to in a later chapter.) For now, suffice to say the doctor didn't stay in the picture for long.

But after I recovered enough from my intense fall, I realized they had given me a pretty cool-looking certificate for making the jump. This was very exciting to me. I was eager to show it to others. I went to work the following Monday and took along the paper to show everyone—"Look what I did!"

I had much more confidence when both of my feet were on the ground. When others saw my certificate, news spread fast. Soon everyone at work knew that Esther had gone skydiving. It didn't take long for the questions and comments about the experience to come my way.

I fielded everything really well. I told them what a thrill it was, how I loved my certificate, and on and on. The attention was great— until several individuals told me they wanted to go skydiving too. And since I was creating an impression that I had done it and loved it, they naturally turned to me. Before I knew it, I was part of a group that was going to go skydiving over the following weekend.

Let's just say that round two wasn't any better than the first time out! Again, I acted all tough at the beginning of the experience. Again, once we were in the plane, my nerves went out of control. When the time came to jump, they had to push me out of the airplane door. I felt beyond numb when I finally hit the ground.

Now, do you think I learned my lesson after this time? Perhaps under normal conditions, as in not-right-after-a-divorce times, I would not have agreed to that second skydiving incident.

But I was actually getting over a divorce and not thinking clearly. So I took my second diploma to work the following week. I showed it around like I had done the first time. Pretty soon I was getting brought into another skydiving outing! I would have to go up for Round 3!

This time, I overplayed my part to the extreme on the way up. I talked to the instructor about fancy moves I had seen in the 007 movies and acted like I was interested in trying them. As a result, when it came time to do the jump, my instructor tried to show me how to do the acrobats! I was strapped to him, and he made us turn and move in the air! I thought I was going to die! I was so out of it that I couldn't respond to him anymore, and the instructor grew concerned.

On the way down, everything grew fuzzier than it had during the previous attempts. In the haze of my consciousness, I could hear the instructor talking into a microphone. He started calling people and asking for help on the ground. He thought I would require medical attention when we arrived.

I definitely needed help! But more than anything, I had to stop skydiving. That time, after three rounds of terror, I left my diploma at home. I didn't take it to work the following week and brag about it. I decided it was time to retire as a skydiver! Three is a charm!!

Keeping Your Word

As I referenced, to this day my children bring up the skydiving incidents and wonder what came over me. I joke that I was suicidal, and it's likely true that I was a bit out of my mind during those months. Still, I like to point out to them that I kept my word. I said I would go skydiving, and I did.

Your challenges may not be skydiving (I hope they aren't! Mostly because my heart still races at the thought of having to fall from the sky!). But no matter the context, I believe it's a good goal to stick to your word, even when it means going through a difficult situation. Others take note of your ability to follow through and they appreciate your accountability.

When I look back on those days, I don't regret keeping my word. I'm satisfied with my decisions to push through and do the hard things, even when they didn't go as smoothly as I would have liked... the experience tested every single cell in my body! Furthermore, I learned about when to press the "pause" button. I validated that skydiving is not for me. Rather than continue that streak of showing off the skydiving certificate, I realized that the sheet of paper could simply get tucked away in my office at home. I didn't need to brag about it at work. I just had to move on with my life (and since then, I have always said "no" to skydiving!). Then I took on white water rafting (but let's leave this story for another time!).

During the following years, I found opportunities to do exactly that—keep pushing forward on my path, both in life and in my career. It was worth it to knock on doors, even when it seemed like they would never open. As I moved forward, I learned how important it is to maintain dignity, even when times get tough. And as we saw in my skydiving memories, keeping your word shows that you are able to commit to something and see it through. In business, as in life, others will appreciate your ability to finish what you set out to do.

In the next compound, we'll look at ways to take on big projects, even when the end isn't easily visible. I'll talk about how to leap into a challenge, tackle it, and learn lessons as you find a solution. Just like skydiving, it might not be easy at the time, but I live with no regrets, and I'm always thankful I accepted the hard task. That said, I'm glad those skydiving days are behind me! Now they only come out in memories and occasional family or friends teasing sessions, when I do a comedy show of the whole story.

Questions for Reflection

- What crazy or audacious things have you done during certain phases of your life marked by high stress?

- As you reflect on these wild memories, what makes you smile? What parts cause you to cringe?

- What lessons have you learned from these outside-of-the-box moments?

- Were there specific reasons that drove your behavior? Were the incidents an offshoot of a deeper personal issue or tough family environment?

- How easy is it to keep your word when times get tough? Are there aspects about accountability in your life that you would like to improve on?

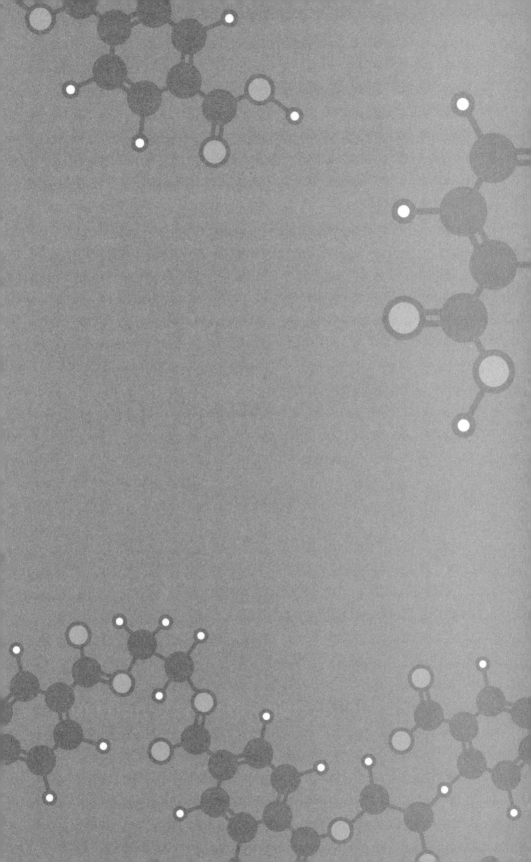

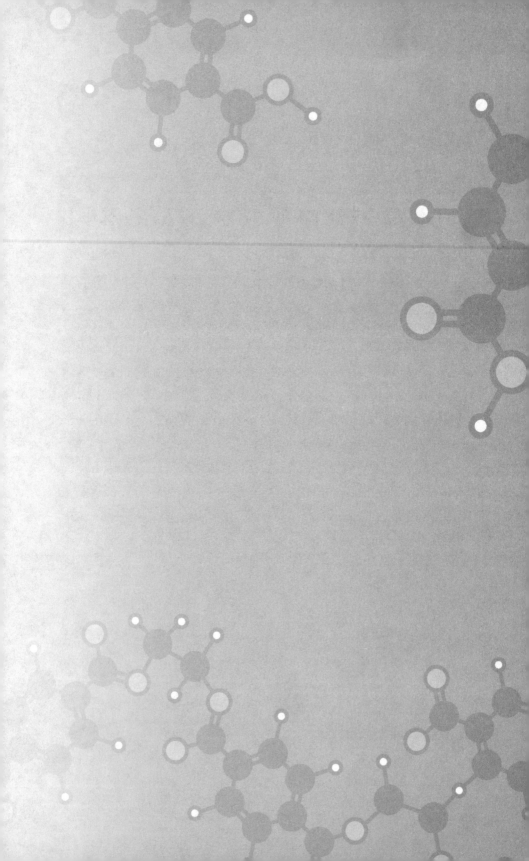

COMPOUND FOUR

Have No Excuses

When someone presents me the chance to challenge myself and learn something new, I just can't resist. I know it will be a way for me to grow as a person. I'll have a way to meet new people and see how they carry out certain processes and approach issues. Through it all, I know I'll have a great time. There's always something to appreciate, to laugh about, and to see in a lighthearted way.

Throughout my career, I've seen, time and again, how having no excuses can lead to amazing opportunities. For me, it opened the pathway to spend time in Denmark and learn about the country. While I was there, I found ways to do even bigger things than I first imagined. I simply saw a need and decided my team could get it done! I believed in them and they rose to the occasion.

That doesn't mean it was simple or easy. I found myself working all day (and night!) and adjusting to a new culture. I had to learn how other workforces approached their jobs, especially in countries with different policies for hours and vacation. I watched distinct leadership styles, and observed individuals take on roles that I would never have assigned them on my own.

But in the end, I was so thankful to see how others get their work done and approach management. I grew as a person during my time in

Denmark. And the experience made me further commit to my goals of being an amazing grandma (trust me, just about everyone wants me to be part of my family!). I continue to cultivate my relationships, and love to keep in touch with people that I've spent time with, and have become like my own family, throughout our years together.

In the next chapters, join me in reflecting on how great it can be to look for ways to say "yes." I didn't always know how it would work out—and you might not either. However, these experiences give us a chance to grow. They can help you build out your own version of being a Poly-Esther. When you keep an attitude that looks for ways to get things done, there is so much potential for what will happen. And like me, you'll have a great time along the way as long as you're open to change and don't take yourself too seriously. I know I don't!

CHAPTER TEN
The Ever Uncomfortable

First, the good news: after five years of blind dates, I found someone to marry. Interestingly, my now-husband Carlos spent years trying to fix me up with others. We never considered the possibility of becoming more than friends for a long time.

That changed, however, when he went through a divorce of his own. I recommended him the books I had gone through when I split from my first husband. One thing led to another, and we started looking at each other differently. We have two very different personalities: I am a risk taker, I move like lightning, and I prefer to approach everything with humor; he is more serious, steady, and appreciates the chance to talk about things without seeing the lighter side in situations.

Now, more than twenty-five years into our marriage, I can say we both feel lucky. We've never raised our voices to each other or had a heated argument. We talk about our disagreements and different points of view and compromise. (Remember this as you read on, because I think you'll be interested in our interactions when I accepted a foreign assignment on the spot!)

While it's great to have stability at home, I have always found that I thrive on challenges in my profession. To grow and develop, the climb up the staircase doesn't have to be completely vertical. For instance, I had a role at the director level in a company and left it when I started to work for another company. There I accepted a position as an associate director, which might seem like a step down. I knew that I would grow there, however, and was promoted to the director level of quality assurance and quality control. Then I was offered a position to move to manufacturing—a new area for me—at the director level. These moves became fundamental for me, as they helped me get moved to become vice president and plant manager of an entire operation in the RTP-NC area. There may be side steps that provide the right kind of learning experience we seek. That's exactly what happened to me when I was asked to go to Denmark.

As you read about this request, I invite you to think about the chances you have been given to uplevel your skills or develop a specific niche. It could be that working on a project allows you to grow in a new area. Even if you don't earn more by taking it on, it could be a way to invest in your long-term future and career. When a promotion opportunity comes later, you'll have a deeper knowledge base to present and use, which could help you move up at that time.

Happy and Settled

Remember the story of my house burning down in chapter 7? By this point, my life had a very different landscape. I had remarried and was living a much more stable life with Carlos, the "monk," as my family calls him. I was working as the vice president of manufacturing and as the general manager of the largest biopharmaceutical manufacturing facility of a global company. Under my watch, the production levels of the site had increased, and we had successfully implemented new technology. I was becoming more known in the C-Suite executive level, partly because of the achievements I had accrued during my four years in the position.

Then one day, my boss called me in to his office. He explained to me that he needed a leader to go to Denmark to oversee a global project. The company had a commitment to build a facility there. "I would love for you to be the one to do that start-up," he added.

I am sure that my boss thought it was a long shot, and that it would be hard to get me to go to Denmark. Carlos and I had just bought a new house. My kids were both grown at that time, and they had children of their own, and I was heavily involved in the lives of my grandchildren.

But it wasn't a hard sell at all. I immediately replied, "Yes, count on me."

And ... I forgot to ask my husband about it first—oops!

It was an honest mistake. I think I was enthralled with the possibility of taking on a new challenge. I love the chance to learn something new. This was an area that I didn't have experience in, which made it especially appealing. I am built to be a "yes" person, especially when it involves something I haven't done before.

The position wouldn't technically be considered a move up. I was a vice president in North Carolina, and I would be a vice president in Denmark. I had been a plant manager in North Carolina, and I would be carrying out that same role in Denmark.

Unfortunately, as you'll recall from those skydiving episodes, I keep my word when I give it! So I had committed to going. I just hadn't told my family or looked at my calendar yet.

For obvious reasons, I had to approach Carlos, and the sooner the better. When I told him, I began by saying, "I think I screwed up." I started out very sad, and in fact, I did have mixed emotions about the change of plans.

My husband saw my state of mind and immediately was sympathetic. He asked me to explain what had happened. "I am sure we can work through this together," he said.

I shared the story of my boss asking me to go to Denmark. I said that the opportunity had been put before me and that I had jumped on it. I had agreed to oversee the facility in Europe but hadn't taken the time to reflect on the consequences of that decision and how it would impact those around me.

When I finished, my husband said, "That's great." Then almost in wonder, he asked, "Am I going too?"

"I'm not going without you," I insisted.

As it turns out, the company gave him a position in Denmark as well (he is in the same industry). This time, I didn't have to knock on hundreds of doors to make the job offer available for him. I was thankful for the support of others in the company, and that they made it possible for us to be in Denmark together.

With those steps, arrangements were made for my husband. Between the two of us, we were on the same page and committed to making the move. Carlos even celebrated the fact that I had been given such a great opportunity. After settling everything at home, I still needed to sort through my kids and the grandkids.

I had become a grandparent at the age of forty-two, and I took that role very seriously. I would often visit the grandchildren or have them stay with me. My husband and I took vacations with them, put them in camps near our home, visited them, and were very involved in their lives. I wasn't sure how I would make it work in Denmark.

After some thought, I wondered if I could prioritize the grandchildren visits while I was in Denmark and thus maintain our close relationship with them. I got creative and found summer camps and programs that they could attend while staying with us in Denmark.

For example, I came up with ways for my granddaughter Carmella to come and be with me for four to six weeks at a time and still continue her studies. An American teacher, who was the wife of my Director of Engineering in the Denmark project and lived nearby, helped me manage a curriculum and cover educational courses so the children could visit and continue their studies.

I was thrilled to go. Had I stayed in my comfortable home, with the routines and schedules, I might have run the risk of getting bored. Let me assure you, there were no lulls in Denmark! And I loved that about the place. In the next chapter, we'll take a closer look at life there.

For now, I encourage you to spend some time thinking of growth and development projects you might pursue. I always tell people that if you have a chance to go abroad, take it! You'll learn so much along the way. Those lessons can be applied to your personal and professional life. Oh, and with the right attitude, you'll have loads of fun along the way too. (I know I did! Tune in to the next chapter for stories about coffee, salsa, and books in Denmark!)

Questions for Reflection

- Have you ever been offered a position that you turned down because it didn't sound like a promotion?
- What are some ways you could evaluate your next career opportunities?
- Are you being challenged in new ways in your current role?
- Have you ever visited, studied, or worked in a different country?
- What benefits would a global outlook provide for your career?
- What goals do you have for your personal growth? How might those get carried out?

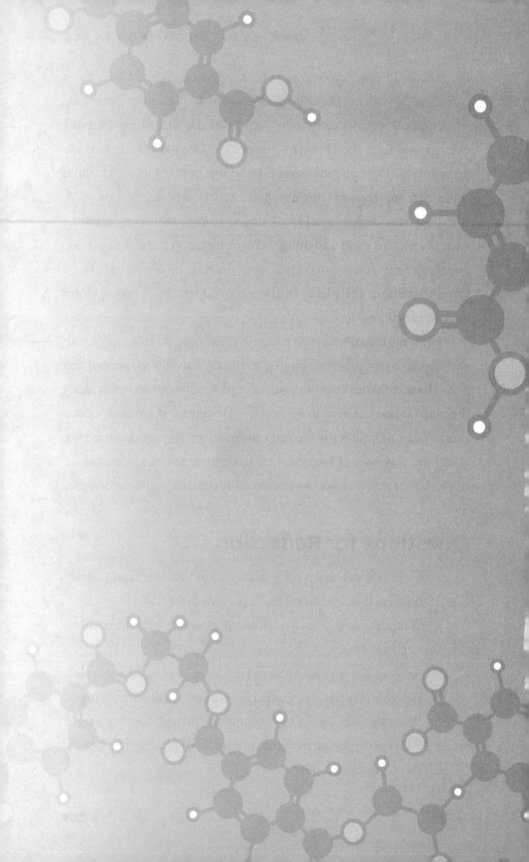

CHAPTER ELEVEN
The Adaptable One

When I arrived in Denmark, it was October. I had come as winter neared and the temperatures dropped, and my first impression of the country was that it was cold. And dark.

In many ways, the move seemed like the ultimate mismatch. Here I was, a Latina in Denmark. After growing up in Puerto Rico and living in places like North Carolina and Hawaii, the weather shock was sudden—and severe. The days were short, the nights were long, and the land was … frigid.

That coolness ran through more areas than a lightweight jacket. In Denmark, I encountered a different rhythm to work, lifestyles, and leadership. At first, I noticed the distinctions in a big way. It was as if I were sitting and watching a play, and these differences took front and center stage. Toward the end of my two years there, however, I had grown to appreciate these styles. In fact, I leaned into them, learning to accept them and draw out their benefits.

A story of my life would not be complete without a glimpse into my time in Denmark. In this chapter, I'll begin with an overview of my start there (get ready for some fun times!). As you read, I encourage you to think about your own life and opportunities. Perhaps you've had the chance to witness other ways of doing things, either close to home or far away. I've seen how every place has something to offer—we only need to be open to it and not afraid to try it out.

New Work Patterns

Coming to Denmark, I had been accustomed to the "all-work-no-life" habits so deeply engrained in the US culture. That didn't mean vacations were nonexistent (and I took all my vacation days, which I'll talk about more in chapter 14), but I was used to long hours and had always been willing to put in extra time to make sure deadlines were met. In the past, I had loved leading teams that had a similar mindset.

With that background, you can imagine my amazement when I arrived in Denmark and learned the rules of the country. For starters, the accepted work week consisted of thirty-five hours, compared to the forty-hour baseline of the United States. Also, on the island of Puerto Rico, when I was growing up there it was expected that employees would not leave until the boss was finished and ready to depart for the day.

But this was not the case in my new European landscape. Employees not only worked shorter weeks; they also expected to be given the time off that the law allotted them. They were to receive a minimum of six weeks' paid vacation every year—and three of those weeks were to be taken together. Holiday time, it seemed, was going to be an ever-present topic.

How were we going to do this? I wondered. I was supposed to lead a group to get FDA and EMA (European Medicinal Agency) approval for the new biomanufacturing site and for manufacturing one of the most efficacious multiple sclerosis drug therapies. This would require complex processes and we had to comply with tight timelines to meet the projected milestones. I was envisioning hours and hours of overtime to get everything done. Instead, I was walking into a scheduling system that seemed to me to be full of vacation days!

Getting It Done

Though the worker availability seemed to be reduced, I soon found bright spots. During working hours, the Denmark facility was quiet! There was no buzz of people talking. Even in the hallways, silence reigned. Here's why: everyone was working! And they took those minutes seriously. They did not stop and chat with coworkers as they passed them. No one spent the first twenty minutes of their day socializing before they started the tasks at hand. In short, they used those thirty-five hours of labor each week … to be productive.

When it was time for lunch, you would find people talking. They were on break and used that time to catch up with others. There was a clear separation between working hours and time off. I found that workers generally struck a balance. They focused on their projects during working hours, and when work was done or they were on break, they put their attention on other things, like finding out what everyone did over the weekend and checking their social media.

It was a clever system—and it was effective. I soon found that productivity didn't suffer. In fact, the built-in rest seemed to provide the energy needed to carry out tasks in a timely manner. I eventually told others that we were going to provide a healthy competition for our peers in the United States! The Danish could demonstrate that working less could actually lead to an increase in efficiency given their work ethics and productivity mindset. At work, this value shone through in teamwork settings and the never-ending removal of "waste time" in all processes. Group participation and involvement was important, and accomplishments were always credited to the team, rather than the individual.

Boosting the Economy with Parking Tickets

Like the Danish people I met, when I'm working, I'm very dedicated. Perhaps a trait that is not so similar is that on my time off I love to shop.

Part of this is practical. There are often errands to run and basic supplies to get. Of course, I love to explore and compare prices at different places too. For me, it's the full experience—browsing can be just as relaxing and reenergizing as coming home with new merchandise.

In Denmark, I found it difficult to shop during the workweek. I often put in double shifts, as I would meet with the European team during the morning sessions, then I would dedicate afternoons and evenings to calls from the US team. I usually took Saturdays and Sundays off, which would have been great for shopping, except that many places in Denmark close on Saturday afternoons. They are also shut down for all of Sunday.

I was coming from a consumerism-based culture, and I was not used to such limited shopping on the weekends! I set my schedule so that on Saturdays I would wake up and clean in the morning, and then I would try to run out in the afternoon to get all the shopping done before everything closed. One time I arranged a weekday so that I would have more time to spend in a store picking out furniture. I drove to the retailer, parked, and then went inside.

Now, in Denmark the parking lots are managed by separate entities, so the store I visited was not in charge of the parking area. Unaware of this nuance, I looked through the store, took my time, found what I wanted, and came back to the car. I had spent three and a half hours inside the place.

To my surprise (and dismay!), there was a parking ticket attached to my vehicle. Apparently, there was a limit on how long vehicles could be parked at the shopping mall. I had greatly exceeded the time frame!

The next week at work, I shared my story with the team. They gave me knowing looks and slowly explained the limits for parking. They went on to add that if I had wanted more time, I should have gone to the car after two hours, moved the vehicle to a different area, and continued my shopping. This would have prevented the ticket.

I think that others in my circles there never quite understood my shopping decision-making process. They found it difficult to understand why I might need an excess of three hours. They thought I stayed in the stores for an unreasonably long period. There was one place called Magasin that I especially loved. I told the others, "Even if I am not buying, I like to go and see."

Over time, I came to a better understanding of Danish culture and norms. I learned that the people there place high values on intangibles like relationships and traveling the world. It was common to have stores closed on Sundays so that families and friends could have social get-togethers. After a few months, I realized my administrative assistant was often jetting off to places over the weekend or on holidays. She might be in London for several days on her time off and in Egypt during the next break. There was a cultural emphasis on travel and experiences in that sense.

This idea of being in places and spending hours with people was meaningful to me. It helped me reflect on my own consumerism background. Time is valuable, memories last forever, and experiences change views. It caused me to think about my values related to relationships. For my grandchildren, I shifted away from sending gifts and instead gave them experiences with me. Together we established memories that we could keep close to our hearts and hopefully change us for the better. I especially focused on their summer times and used their breaks as opportunities to offer them meaningful learning experiences, although, I must admit, it was less expensive to give a present like a toy or electronic set than to take the family on a vacation trip!

Quiet Leadership

Besides the start-up of the drug substance biomanufacturing site launch efforts that I was leading in Denmark, the site had a smaller but important operation in the drug distribution supply chain. This operation conducted drug label and packing for distribution to clinical trials and device assembly for auto-injectors, which were commercial products. Not long after I entered the scene, there was a crisis at the device assembly operations. The production of a commercial auto-injector was in jeopardy, and its commercial launch was put on hold.

Further complicating the matter, the director of operations moved to a new position. I was left to sort things out and answer the many phone calls coming in as others asked about the status of the device assembly operation, which was keeping the launch of the new auto-injector on hold. Many salespeople and executives were planning on a date that had been set, and they were now worried that the deadlines wouldn't be met. They wanted to know why.

I had never received so many phone calls in a day as I did during the crisis! We looked for a replacement for the director that left as a way to help carry on. I knew it was essential to bring on a leader who could properly fill the site head and director role.

Which type of leader do you think Esther wanted to see in the vacant position? I'll tell you: someone just as energetic as me! Since I am full of life, I am naturally drawn to others who are enthusiastic. When the candidate list was formed, I found someone who looked perfect.

He was vivacious, ambitious, and demonstrated an eagerness to move mountains … in short, he was just like me!

Another candidate was in the mix, and this person was quiet as a mouse. *How could he possibly lead?* I thought. No one will listen to him, let alone notice him. A quiet leader would be the exact opposite of my style.

There was one problem, though. When it came time to choose from the pool of possibilities and hire a new director, I saw that others didn't share my opinion. Among the group that was making the selection, I was in the minority in favoring the less quiet candidate. Most wanted to see the quieter applicant get hired, and they voted accordingly.

At this point, I had several options. I could have spoken up and defended my thoughts on who would be the better leader. I also could choose to not fight the battle and see what happened. In the end, I decided to let the matter go and listened to the others. They thought the mild-mannered candidate would be the better fit.

I wasn't sure what would happen next. During the months that followed, I kept an eye on the new director and got to know him. I watched him take the reins and carry out his duties. Moreover, I saw him gain respect from others. When he opened his mouth to speak, people listened. He knew how to speed up turnaround times and increase efficiencies. If we had to fire someone, he would get the job done—and not even blink once.

Within six months, I was no longer questioning the decision. On the contrary, I was on my knees, giving thanks that he was serving as the new director. I was so glad that I had listened to the opinion of others. The man who got the job was so thoughtful and brought a certain dynamic to leadership that I hadn't seen before—and it was exactly what the company and these operations needed at the time. In a matter of a few months, he was able to pull together a diverse team of expertise to correct the device assembly technical issue and increase the operations productivity to the highest levels ever.

My biggest lesson learned during that time is that diversity is not just gender or ethnicity, but it includes leadership styles. For the first time in my life, I thought about the advantages that come from being a "quiet" leader. This new leader had a way about him that worked for the situation, and I greatly respected him for that. It made me more receptive to other styles of management that differed from my own but were still effective.

Questions for Reflection

- What types of work culture have you participated in? Do you have preferences for one style or another?
- Have you ever come across an individual in the workplace who seemed to be the exact opposite of you? How did you react?
- Are there times when you've benefited from following a group decision, even if you weren't sure about it at the time?
- What benefits do you see in having diverse leadership teams? Have you been part of a team with players from all over? What were the results of this involvement?

CHAPTER TWELVE
The "Yes Woman"

During my two years in Denmark to carry out the FDA and EMA approval-based project, an interesting situation arose. I learned that my company was working on a new venture with another firm. While my organization was US-based, this other firm had headquarters in South Korea. The two corporations wanted to work together to produce four drug therapy products for various rare diseases.

Here's the twist: they were going to outsource the work out to a third party. They felt our company did not have an available site to make this happen. The US sites seemed impractical because they were already at maximum capacity and utilization of their resources. Denmark wasn't a candidate because they were too busy with the site start-up and approval of the one commercial drug therapy for multiple sclerosis.

I looked at what they wanted in the new venture. I reviewed the plans for the four drug therapies. Then I came up with an idea of my own. I decided to present it and see what would happen.

With that goal in mind, I approached the leaders of this new venture. After reviewing the project, I asked them, "Why are you going to contract this away?" Before anyone could answer, I added, "We can do it here in Denmark."

In short, I had said "yes" before even being asked the question. It seems I was advancing from my earlier days! Back in North Carolina, when I had been asked to come to Denmark, I had agreed without even consulting my husband. Now I was here, offering to take on new challenges before they were brought to me!

I'm glad I did. You see, my motivation for doing it wasn't purely self-driven. I could see that bringing in more work would be hugely advantageous to the group of employees under my care and supervision in Denmark. As I told them, "Look, you are working on getting approval for one drug. If anything goes wrong, this whole plant could close down." It was definitely a possibility, and it would mean that the workers could lose their jobs. I knew this would be difficult for them, especially for those who loved their line of work—and their families could face hardship, too.

Instead, I proposed bringing on the manufacturing of the new products for the rare diseases to the operations in Denmark. "Think about it," I explained to the workers. "If these four new products stay here, we will prolong the chances of this plant staying open for you and your kids. This other FDA and EMA approval we're currently working on only represents one commercial drug for your facility. If something happens to it, you'll have to close."

Then I explained my big "why" behind my offer (yes! a "why" bigger than the facility potentially closing!). I told the employees, "If I thought you weren't capable, I wouldn't have suggested it. But I offered to produce these drugs here because I know you are able to do this and more."

That's all they needed to hear. Soon I got everyone on board. We figured out a way to organize so that we could divide up the workload. One group would focus on the FDA and EMA approval, and the others would implement the production needed for the four additional drugs.

If there was ever a time in my life when I was sure people thought I was crazy, it was then. I knew that my boss trusted my judgment, but others were shaking their heads. They must have thought that I was putting into jeopardy the completion of the main project I went to Denmark for. The Denmark site was already busy working toward the FDA and EMA approval. It could easily come across to others that I was taking on too much by adding four new products. They likely thought that we wouldn't be able to fulfill our commitments.

Agreeing with the Complaints

When I urged operations to send more production to Denmark, I knew we could do it. But at the same time, we were overworked already. The FDA and EMA approval process was rigorous, and we had too much on our plates before anything else arrived.

As you might guess, the onslaught of so many jobs led to issues—and lots of them. I knew effective communication would help to calm the anxieties and fears that ran rampant. I spent some time thinking about best ways to listen to feedback. I couldn't have a conversation with each person every day, but I could set up a system so that everyone felt heard.

With that purpose in mind, I established a series of roundtables and carried out discussions almost every day in the facility. I shared with groups that I knew we were growing so fast that we couldn't keep up. New hires were needed and that would take time. But in the meantime, everyone had more than they could handle. I told all participants in the roundtable discussion that I wanted to be accessible and hear from them how they were doing.

At each meeting, I let the individuals vent for fifteen to twenty minutes. They typically shared that they had too much to do; they mentioned they didn't have the tools to get everything done. During this time, I listened intently.

Then I would turn the discussion and express empathy. I wanted to direct their attention to what was important, and I routed them to my personal situation to do that. I would share that I understood their pain and that I also was going through a hard time. I would explain how I had left my family behind and was missing my grandchildren terribly. I would add that I never imagined coming to Denmark would mean working a day shift and a night shift (since I had to take meetings to accommodate US working hours). Then I would continue and say, "I am determined that we will get through this. Once we get the facility up and running, it will have meaning in your life and the life of your kids."

Through these conversations, I would get them to see a future and the benefits they would personally receive from getting through the difficult next steps. I listened carefully for the bottlenecks they were pointing out. I knew that my main job was to make my employees' job easier to execute. We re-prioritized activities and brought on the appropriate resources.

This strategy usually helped the workers focus on the tasks at hand, so I would share updates on what we were doing and how we would be getting more assistance. They would give ideas to me too. I would take notes as they spoke. "That's fantastic," I would say if an ingenious thought was shared. "I am glad you are telling me that."

At that time, I was overseeing about six hundred people in the facility. I made groups of ten to twelve people for each roundtable discussion. That way, I could touch everybody in the operation. I would hear directly from the people who were in the trenches, so to speak.

Learning to Drive

Being new to the country, not speaking the same native language, and spearheading such a complex project was like walking a tightrope. I knew I needed to gain everyone's trust. If I could not build strong relationships, it was going to be a rough time for us all.

So I kept listening. And I listened some more. As people opened up to me, I realized there was an underlying fear that rippled through the plant. Team members were unsure about making decisions. Carefree spirits and independent thinking did not exist, at least not vocally during meetings.

Workers in Denmark knew the headquarters for the company were located in the United States. They saw this center across the ocean as the ultimate authority. If an important issue was brought to the table, I often was told, "We have to wait until 2:00 p.m. That's when the United States wakes up."

I knew that if we took that approach, we were running a great risk. We were trying to get the crucial stamp of government approval. So much was at stake, including the very future of the facility and its workers. If we could get the approval, it would be a huge step forward for everyone. But to reach that point, we would have to make more proactive decisions on our side.

I decided to explain the situation with a metaphor. I told the group, "Think of it like a road trip. Our leaders in the United States need us to meet them at a certain destination and have given us a Cadillac to get there. The vehicle is built and ready to go, but the car can't arrive there without us. We have to get in the driver's seat and drive it there."

In this way, I was showing them that *they* could steer the "car"— our project—to keep it on the road. They could avoid potholes and debris. If a detour came up, they could take it and get back on the route later. Leadership trusted them to make these decisions and course correct, because they couldn't be there on the course with them. By empowering them to make these maneuvers on their own, we could enable team members to not only make progress but also feel more confident.

As the months passed, I watched more employees move into the driver's seat. They were ready to have a voice and share their opinions. They knew how to look out for the project and help us meet the much-needed milestones. This change made it possible to keep that FDA and EMA approval in sight: We would make it if we stood up and worked together.

In both cases—taking on the heavier workload and encouraging others to take initiative—the results were positive. We were able to stay on track with all lines of production. The group in Denmark started to see how they could play a bigger role and make decisions too.

Through it all, the driving force was centered on a willingness to take a chance. Saying "yes" even before being asked, and motivating others to take the reins, went a long way. As I look back, I have no regrets. After all, rather than sitting down and letting opportunities pass by, I was ready to jump and try. And when I did, others followed along. Together we worked to make a difference.

Questions for Reflection

- When have you had the chance to say "yes" to an opportunity? How did you respond? Are you happy with your decision?
- Have you ever stood up and volunteered to do something before being asked?

- In what situations would you like to see yourself taking the initiative? Is there a project you've been meaning to take on?
- What strategies could you use to encourage behavioral changes in others, such as helping them to build confidence?
- Are there some tactics you could implement to grow in your own self-confidence?

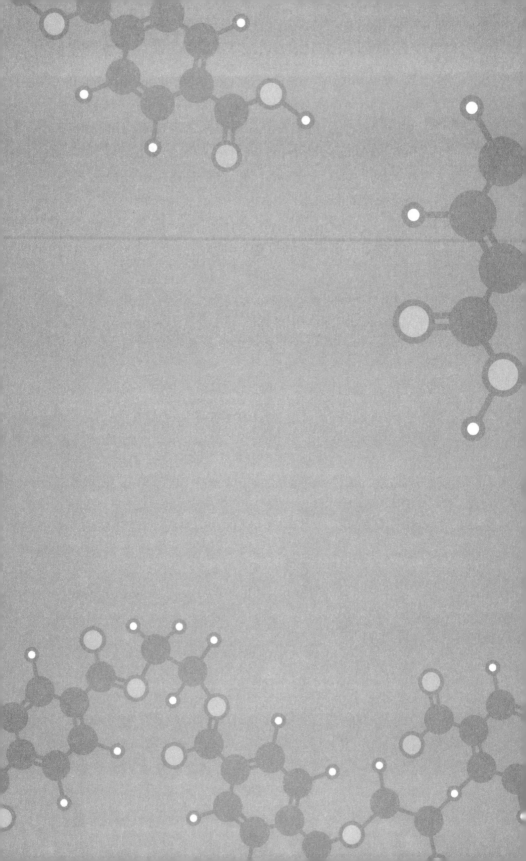

CHAPTER THIRTEEN
The Fun One

I love to dance. I've always looked forward to getting out on the floor and moving to music. These days, I put on bright red lipstick once a week. I pull on my favorite workout clothes, and I head to a Zumba class—which I love—to teach.

That's right (by now you know I am full of surprises!), I am a Zumba instructor and I put together routines for my group to follow. Every class I get a great deal of exercise, as I purposely exaggerate the movements so that everyone else can easily see them and know what they are supposed to do.

When I get home, I crash. I am often sore the next day due to the strain. But the next week, I'm at it again, complete with my outfit and bright lipstick.

Why Zumba? You might ask.

I think, *Why not?*

I love to dance, I love to move, and I love the chance to continue learning. I think that every way we can engage our brain is an opportunity to stay alert, active, and, best of all, to have fun along the way. When I was in Denmark, I found avenues to pursue my passion of great music and rhythm. It's just a part of who I am, and I couldn't help letting it seep into my leadership style too.

Dancing through Denmark

I formed a theory about salsa dancing during my time in Europe. I proposed that Denmark used to be part of the Caribbean and then shifted to the North after the Ice Age. When I shared this idea, people would ask me, "Why do you say that?"

I would reply, "Because you can dance to Latin rhythms like a native!"

It was true. I went to festivals during my time there and couldn't believe the movement I saw! Now, salsa dancing is one of my specialties. While I was abroad, on more than one occasion I went out on a Friday with my husband. We would dress up and get ready to show off some great moves to the beat of live music.

After getting all glamorous, we would head out to Copenhagen with anticipation. However, before hitting the dance floor, we always turned to watch others who were already there. I found myself staring with wide eyes at maestros who looked like they could be in Cuba or Puerto Rico. They had rhythm! And these great moves were so fun to watch.

In the workplace, I couldn't resist bringing in a bit of this lively movement. I had a cowbell that I kept at hand. We had monthly meetings during which I would deliver updates and present the site project metrics. If we reached a milestone and/or met all the timelines for the month, it would call for a recognition. I would ring the cowbell by playing a salsa tune. Before long, everyone was clapping and moving with me. Soon, every time that I rang the cowbell and played the salsa tune they would exclaim, "More! More! More!" I would do the dance sounds and movement again for them.

Celebrating Milestones with Music

I never imagined I would incorporate my love of salsa with the joint venture our company had with a South Korean firm. But, as it turns out, I did find a way to bring in some music. I think the others involved were just as surprised as me with the outcome.

During the time we took on the venture with the South Korean company, I ran into some challenges that I found could be resolved with a little collaboration—and a lot of laughter. We had regular meetings with the leadership of the other company. Sometimes these discussions took place in South Korea, and sometimes they occurred in Denmark.

In between these gatherings, I would occasionally get word that all was not well between the Europe and Asia departments. I would say, "What's going on?"

They would reply, "We don't know what to say. They ask us a question and we answer. Three days later they ask us the same question and we give the same answer."

I thought about this repetitive conversation and wondered if there was more below the surface. I formed a theory that the Asian company, which operated in a hierarchal manner, was not getting the answer they thought they were supposed to receive.

I decided to get on the phone and call up the leadership there. After some small talk, I touched on the more pressing topic. "You're not getting what you want," I mentioned during our conversation. The person on the other end explained what they were looking for, and then I understood the situation better. I suggested a compromise and did a bit of negotiating. By the end of our chat, the other side had agreed to accept different terms and I had offered to make some changes at the facility in Denmark.

I went back to the team and explained that we had found a middle ground. I added that in the future it would be wise to take their culture into consideration. "Don't think they aren't listening," I said. "If they ask again, it's likely because they want to hear a different answer. Next time they ask a question for the second time, respond with a message that says, 'What do you wish the outcome were?'"

Working small issues out like this had positive outcomes, and it helped us build that relationship. Before long, members of the South Korean company were coming to visit our facility on a monthly basis. On one occasion, the South Korean company CEO came for a tour. He even attended one of my bell ringing sessions (an event usually lasted about thirty minutes). In it, I recognized the site for meeting milestones.

The CEO stood next to me as I began that session. When it came time to ring the cowbell and start the salsa tune, it occurred to me to have him do it. Without hesitation, I turned to him and handed him the cowbell. At first, he didn't know what to do. But I knew that his community and culture loved salsa music, so I told him, "Salsa." He agreed and went with the flow.

The place erupted with applause. The workers were thrilled. He looked at me in near shock, as if to say, "That was awesome!" There we were, a mixing of four cultures—Puerto Rican, South Korean, American, and Danish. We found some common ground with a little clapping and some dancing.

Those same principles can be applied to other cultures too. I always say that if we can laugh together, we can get through anything. It really makes a difference. It lightens the mood and helps everyone embrace being together.

Beyond the Surface

Certainly, laughter has its place. There may be times when it's best to put the jokes aside. That said, if you know me, you can be sure that there will be funny things that happen when we are together. It's just how I am. And I think that fun times can help us bond on deeper levels. Humor is often used to drive home significant points. That's exactly what happened later in Denmark.

That cowbell I would ring? I kept using it as we reached our milestones. When the FDA visited our facility, they gave us the much-anticipated approval. In addition, the EMA came and passed us too. So did other secondary markets and countries that did their own inspections. We got approval for everything.

I knew we had to do something to celebrate this incredible accomplishment. I decided we had to throw a party. On the occasion, I gave a speech and explained that we were going to graduate from the use of the cowbell to the use of the official company bell. We selected an employee to ring the company bell. Executives were there, cheering along with us. I told them, "From now on, we will use an official company bell. It was a true effort from everyone that was behind this project. I knew you could do it—and you did."

When my time there came to an end, the group presented me with a book they had made for my time there, complete with funny stories and memories titled *"Prinsessen på Hottet."* They also acted it out for me. They presented me with a large frame with a photo that displayed the Danish employees in front of the site, each holding flags from the United States, Denmark, and Puerto Rico!! I left on a note that is hard to describe: we had been through so much together, and we came out not only successful but laughing. Perhaps that was the biggest sign of success.

Questions for Reflection

- What is your approach to humor? Are you a person who laughs frequently?
- Are you able to keep a lighthearted approach and laugh at yourself when you make a small mistake?
- How do you typically react when someone tells a joke?
- Have you been in work settings that are so fun they don't feel like "work"?
- What ways would you like to incorporate fun and humor into your everyday life?

CHAPTER FOURTEEN
The One Wearing All the Hats

While I was absorbed with my work in Denmark, I never forgot my family or my other responsibilities. Before my time ended in Europe, I was promoted to Senior Vice President of Global Manufacturing. I went on to leadership positions in Boston after Denmark (so many cold places! I started to wonder if the next place for me would be Alaska!). Still, my professional life and title were only part of the many roles I played at the time.

I would never forget how my grandkids saw me as someone very different from a chemist and business leader. Once, before I went to Denmark, I had an interesting interaction with my oldest grandson. I reflected on it during my time abroad. It happened when he was five years old and I was driving him to a summer camp. You'll remember that I am a very involved abuela, and this was no outlier event. I have a strong relationship with my grandkids, and I'm a little bit proud of that fact (if you haven't noticed!). At the very least, it means I recognize I have worked hard to build ties with them from early on.

During this particular outing, it occurred to me that the little boy might not know much about my job. I asked, "What does your father say about me—did he tell you that you have a smart grandmother?" I presented this question with the understanding that my son may have told his preschooler that I was a doctor, or perhaps a scientist.

"No, no, nothing," came the reply.

Huh, I thought.

"What about your mother? Has she told you that you have a smart grandmother?" I asked.

"No."

What?! I thought in my head. So, I asked, "Have you noticed?"

"No, not really," he responded.

I couldn't believe it. Here I was, holding a PhD and with a long list of titles and innovations to my name, and to this five-year-old, I was merely "Abuela."

I decided to set the record straight. I told him, then and there, that I was a "Doctor." Later in the week, I took him on a walk through the biopharma facility I was managing, and he goggled at the way others treated me. He definitely was seeing his abuela in a different light! He said, "Grandma, you are smart." I was glad to get some family recognition (!).

Today I look back on the incident and laugh. After all, he was young. And kids' perspectives are often funny. The memory also points out how we tend to be different things to different people. Our families see us one way; our coworkers view us in our "job" modes. Those who report to us, along with our superiors, will each have their own idea of who we are. Then there's of course how we see our own selves.

Collectively, these often present a kaleidoscope-like picture. As we turn and move about our day, we take on distinct traits, and people view us in separate capacities. We may be forever changing, but we are the same person at heart. (At least I am! And I'm writing the book, so I'll take advantage of being able to make this point!)

I want to spend some time investigating these various images. How do we carry ourselves? How do we switch off one hat and put on another? What do we have to do to make sure we are holding onto our priorities and values?

I believe there are ways to find a balance—I have worked on it time and again throughout the past decades. What I've found is that it is OK to be a professional, a parent, a grandparent, a friend, a spouse, and part of a family. You can't fully separate those aspects of yourself from each other, and those roles can evolve over time.

As an example, in my family, when I was a child and young adult, I tended to feel like the black sheep. I had older siblings who were smarter, younger siblings who were cuter ... and then there was me. I didn't finish college right away, I got married young, I wasn't successful or wealthy by certain standards—in short, I was the odd one out. When you feel like the odd one out, chances are you don't feel respected to the same degree everyone else is, and I craved respect.

Of course, it's pretty easy now to reflect on that time and see how I changed. Now with a doctorate and various accomplishments in my field, along with innovative projects and a start-up that I'm heading—not to mention my happy and growing family—that feeling has pretty much been smashed to bits! That said, it took time and many steps forward to gain that respect I dreamt of having.

Though my grandson was incredibly young, it surprised me to know that he didn't see me as the full person I was—not just as his abuela but also as the leader and innovator I've worked hard to become. And he wasn't the only person in my life who wasn't seeing the full Esther. Now that he's grown and pursuing engineering, he's of course more aware of what I do. And over the time that's passed as I worked to show others who I fully was and gain that respect I desperately wanted, I gained a greater perspective of my own, too.

I love being a spouse, abuela, a mom, a Zumba instructor, a friend, a biopharma professional, a mentor. But I'm all of those things and then some. The reality that I will never be just one. Like all of us, I carry the responsibilities of not only my career but my family, too. And I hold a commitment to myself to live out my values in each of these areas.

While you can never deny the various parts of yourself, at certain times I do believe in separating these. When I was going through a divorce, for instance, I kept the inner workings of my personal life to myself while I was on the job. I also have made great efforts to ensure that the long hours of my career impact my family as little as possible. When my children were young, I would wake up at 4:00 a.m. to get in work time, or to stay up late and hit the books (or computer) after they were asleep, sometimes watching the clock strike 2:00 a.m. before I headed for bed. Have I been sleep deprived at times? Yes! However, it's always been worthwhile.

And to everyone's benefit, I have learned some best practices from both the personal and professional aspects of my life. I have even taken lessons learned from my home experience and used them at work—and vice versa.

In the following sections, let's decipher this dance, which shows how different components of one's life can complement each other. We'll start by looking at what I've adopted from my parenting to work life. Then we'll have a bit of fun and see how some management techniques in my industry have been applied to my household.

Seeing You as My Child

When I first started my career, I didn't have a manager role and mostly had to look after myself and my projects at work. I took my responsibilities seriously and was always watching how the higher-ups acted. Did they walk through the hall and greet all the workers they saw, or did they hold their salutations until another executive came along? I watched some leaders go to great lengths to ignore the people under them, while others presented strong examples of being open and friendly to everyone.

After watching different styles, I knew that if I ever had a chance to be a leader, I would want to carry out my duties with heart. I had seen everything from leading by example to leading by threats by then, and I had established a plan for myself. So when I was put into management positions, and then became a leader of leaders, I knew I would have to work hard to present myself in a way that reflected my chosen approach.

In many areas, this worked well. People tend to appreciate an honest, open leader who is ready to talk to others at all levels and have discussions. However, I did find that there was one area that was very tough for me to face, and this involved providing feedback. Specifically, sharing details about a person's apparent lackluster performance.

Oh, how I dreaded performance reviews! If the comments that I had to give were positive, then it was, as I like to say, "a piece of cake." The problem came when I had to pass on tough feedback to an individual. I absolutely dreaded it. There was often pain involved on both sides. I didn't like sharing the negative review, and who could blame the receiver for being unenthused by harsh criticism? Further plaguing my dilemma was the fact that I had seen employees spiral into a dark emotional place during these times.

I recall three specific incidents where three talented females lost their own confidence after their respective bosses' harsh criticism. This was not because they could not take objective criticism. Instead, it was due to the communication style and the events that followed. These were too much for them to bear, and they were crushed emotionally.

I realize we all are not made equally and there are different levels of tolerance to harsh criticism. What is extremely important in a leader or leader of leaders is that the criticism be delivered with full respect and from a point of wanting to help the individual. Trust me—if, at the end of the day, you have to make the decision to let the person go, you will sleep like a baby because you did all you could in your power to help.

It can be hard to maintain a good reputation for yourself and the other person when the discussion has to deal with difficult topics. Still, sometimes it had to be done. I found that in these circumstances, it really helped to view the other person as my son or daughter. I would say the same things and go over the hard reviews, but my body language and tone would be different. By treating the employee like a family member, I would be assuring them that we were having this discussion because I wanted to bring the best out of them—not because I wanted to destroy the person.

I should note that there were some extreme instances when even all my best parenting tricks didn't lead to a positive outcome. There will always be moments on the job when someone just doesn't work out. But even through these, I would do all I could to treat them as a parent would handle a situation with a child in which they both want to see a positive outcome and maintain a strong relationship. I let them know that I wanted only the best for them, and that I respected them for who they were. I found that doing so would help to soften the tough conversations we had. My approach would also help me know that I had done all I could to extend a hand to the individual and give them the chance to improve.

Family Meetings with Dr. Mommy

When I took on more managerial roles and then started directing people, group interactions took on a new meaning. If I were at the table leading a meeting, I knew I had to offer guidance and direct it in a certain way so that it would be productive. I had also collected strategies from others that I wanted to model, which included allowing everybody to contribute. I put these into action. Over time, I established my ways of running a meeting and following an agenda.

Turns out, these concepts were very applicable to home life too! Since I was a single mom for years before remarrying, I had to oversee a long list of responsibilities at home. There were chores to carry out, topics to discuss, and schedules to set. I came up with the idea of having a family meeting, complete with some basic rules and an agenda to follow.

I tried it out, and it soon became a staple in my life. It was so much easier to talk about a certain subject as a group if we had it on a list. I also looked for ways to allow the kids to provide feedback, just as I did at work. If we had to clean the house, for instance, we would talk about how it would get done, and who would carry out each task. When Carlos entered my life, he joined in these meetings as well.

This worked so well that I continued it for years. I always ran the discussions and even called myself "Dr. Mommy." There was only one concept that I left out in those family meetings: the performance review. Although looking back, it may have been a good thing to try, especially at Christmas! Imagine if we would have talked at the beginning of the year and then reflected at the end? If you are a parent, you will likely appreciate this idea and the implications it could hold. (It might even save you some money for gifts!)

Setting the Right Priorities

Through it all, I have made sure to have time for the family. When I was given vacation time at work, I always took every single day I was due. I never let it accumulate. I wanted to be there for my children, my grandchildren, my other family members, and my friends.

I decided to build in rules to keep relationships alive and well in my life. I started by marking days on a calendar that were important. Today, I continue that pattern. I note upcoming birthdays and trips, along with holidays and significant events. I pencil in times to send an invitation, a gift, and when to make a phone call.

With this strategy, I set aside time each year to have vacation with my kids and grandkids. I also arrange a trip for my husband and me to take—nobody else is invited on that one! I take a yearly trip with some of my siblings, and they love to laugh as much as me somehow, which means we have fun from the moment we see each other until we bid one another *ciao*. I go away regularly with a set of girlfriends, and my husband and I head out with other couples too. All these are helpful to establish and maintain what I consider to be vital relationships in my life.

When I'm at home, I love to entertain too. It's not uncommon for me to invite someone over, and if they are a new person in my life, I always extend the invitation to my kids too. When they were younger, they would naturally be at home and meet the person. Now that they are adults, I still tell them about the guest and dinner plans, and they are welcome to come.

And yet, there are so many more people I would love to see! There are individuals I first met in places like Fort Bragg, North Carolina, where I spent time after coming to the United States from Puerto Rico. These people became like family to me. The same happened in Hawaii, and I grew close to others there who were very much like me—on their own and far from other relatives. We created our own family.

It isn't possible to see everyone consistently, so I make a big deal for the holidays to get in as many as possible. At Christmas, everybody—and I mean everybody—that I know will receive something from me. I always hold a huge Christmas Eve party, which has become an important family tradition. I invite my kids, their spouses, and the grandchildren of course. Then I bring in my adopted family too. These are people who have come into my life and formed a strong relationship with me—it feels like we are relatives. I have done this gathering for so many years that some of these guests have grown up and are now married with their own families.

The party is so big that everyone looks forward to it, especially the kids. Some of them talk about it all year! And they get ready for it. That's because during the annual event, we hold a talent show for the kids. It's something that I started over a decade ago, and I open it up to anybody who has just been born to anyone who hasn't finished the university yet.

It has become such a big deal that I now make a program for it. I also talk to the kids and their parents beforehand so I can learn what they have accomplished during the last year. This way I can call out some of their achievements during the event.

When it's time for the talent show to start, everyone gathers around. I take the microphone and start with the youngest attendees. I introduce them and share a few things I know about their life—some of these may have been what they mentioned to me, and others might be information I already knew about them. Then I turn and ask the kid, "Do you have a talent?"

And they always answer, "Yes!"

Then I hand them the microphone and let them perform. And wow, how they act! These kids prepare so well for these talent shows. It always amazes me what they are able to learn and do. Personally, it's my favorite part of the whole party.

In addition to the talent show, I always have a program for the ladies which includes a silly gift exchange. Everyone brings a present and then we put them in a pile. Each person gets a chance to open a gift or exchange it for one that someone else has—and it gets wild! I also hold different themed competitions for the men. The entire evening is one long highlight reel. The food and dancing that I incorporate every year help it all come together to create a special time for everyone. In a sense, it's proof of how I have created my own village. I have worked on these relationships and it's important for me to continue building them.

The guests tell me that these times are meaningful for them too. One of my grandsons started performing in the talent show when he was just a baby. At the time, his mother would take him and help him move his hands to clap. Everyone in the room would clap along—that was his talent. He kept participating each year, and by the time he was three, he was acting on his own. When I asked him if he had a talent, he confidently replied, "Yes!" He came and took the microphone and started his performance. He did a stint to the tune of "Baby Shark." Everyone in the audience moved along to the act and applauded him at the end of it.

When the holidays end, we roll into the New Year and carry the memories with us. In January, I always make a lot of phone calls. It might take me the whole month in January, but I go through my list and call everyone I didn't have a chance to see so that we can catch up. I only wish we could see each other face to face more often. But they are very important to me, and I want them to know that.

Without these types of arrangements, it can be easy to let relationships slip. Suddenly decades go by, and you haven't connected. I never want my professional duties to be so demanding that there isn't time to nurture the personal friendships I have developed over the years.

Not long ago, I met up with an old friend from Hawaii. We had first connected when we were in the university there together. She had two kids, like me. Her husband was also in the military, like mine. She was trying to better herself too. Like me, she underwent hard times and even a divorce. And like me, she wanted to continue her studies, ultimately getting her master's degree in chemistry and marrying our organic chemistry professor (who by the way was a Robert Redford lookalike!). So she stayed on the island, but after I left we still kept in touch.

When the two of us finally met again in Hawaii in person (after thirty years of occasional correspondence), we went out to a restaurant. It was like old times again. It was so worthwhile to work on maintaining that relationship. She and I picked up where we left off, just like I know we will the next time our paths cross.

The thing is, all relationships require a time commitment. That's true for work groups and personal ties too. I'm glad I've committed hours to catching up with friends. It may not be the easiest to juggle, but it makes all the difference, just as it has with my friend in Hawaii. Our correspondence helps us stay connected and maintain a close bond, even if the miles greatly separate us.

Questions for Reflection

- What hats do you currently wear at home? At work? In other places?

- Have you ever felt overwhelmed with your roles? What were the outcomes of these times?
- What strategies could you adapt to maintain relationships you care about?
- What type of friendships and lifestyle do you want to have when you step away from your career?

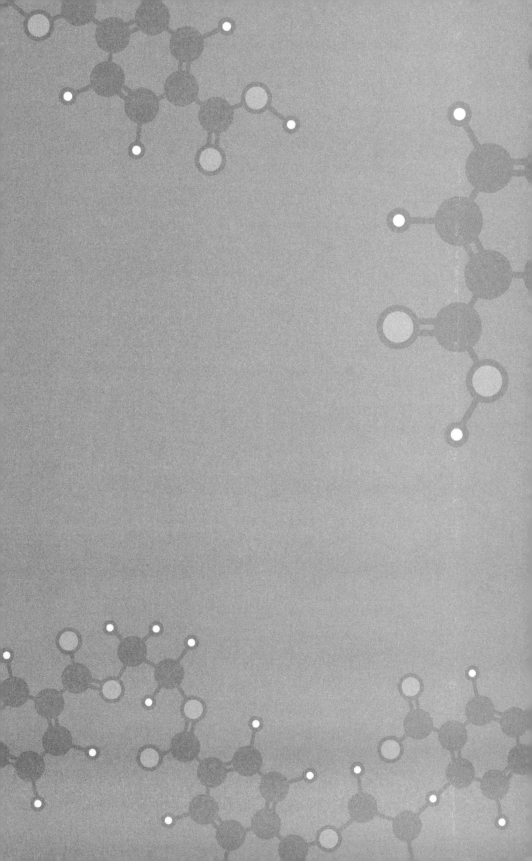

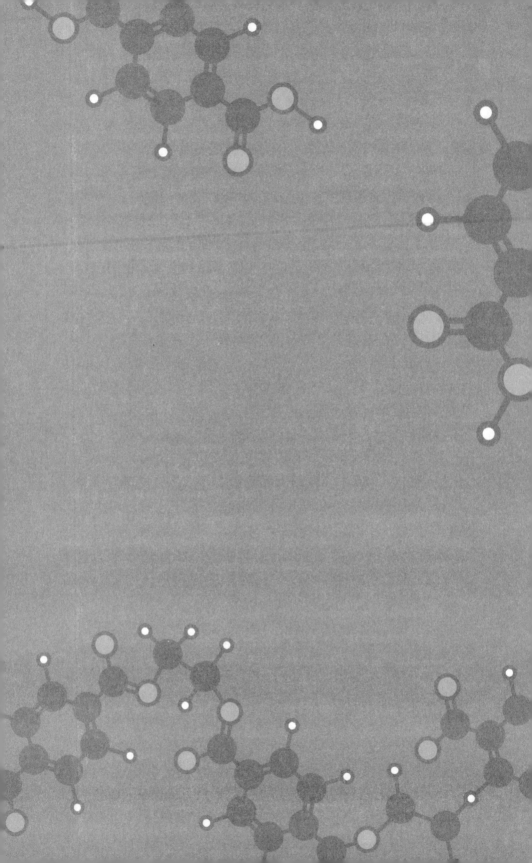

COMPOUND FIVE

Bond with Others

When I stepped away from my full-time career (before I began the start-up in "retirement"), I had four going away parties. After I left the company, people told me that nobody has had as many parties as Esther, not before and not after!

Every time, people at these gatherings would ask me, "What is your legacy?"

Now, I spent decades leading projects and teams in the pharmaceutical industry. I oversaw the completion of drugs and was involved in some pretty great innovations. Surely people were expecting me to list some of these or highlight a few of my favorites.

Instead I said, "I think the legacy I am leaving behind is the next generation of leaders that will step up to the plate. It includes the people that I have seen shine and grow so much in their careers. Every time I saw one of you being promoted, it was like we were both promoted. Your success was really a success for me too."

My inclinations were correct—they were expecting a different speech! One that was full of my achievements and the drugs I have helped to develop. "Oh, yeah, they're important," I agreed. "No question about it. If you would have asked me for my second legacy, I would have answered that way. But you are my main legacy."

I think if you want the title of "leader," you have to be ready to produce and raise the next generation of leaders. And that involves bonding with others in many ways. It includes building relationships with individuals who share different perspectives. It means leaning into the strengths of each generation. It encompasses opening up and sharing with others in ways that can help them on their own path.

It's equally important as a leader to get comfortable with delegating. It's simply not possible to do everything on your own. You'll want to empower your reports. When you master this skill, you'll be able to become a leader of leaders.

That's exactly what we'll look at in the coming chapters. I want to talk about how legacies can be formed. We'll look at ways I've shared my mental health struggles with others to help them overcome their own challenges.

Finally, we'll conclude with some thoughts on what retirement is often portrayed as, and why I prefer a different approach. I encourage you to use these chapters as a way to think about your own path, your own history, your own challenges, the relationships in your life, and your goals. Take everything you can from my own story and apply it to your own—after all, that's part of what I did on my own journey! It is my hope that by the end of the book, you'll have a toolbox ready with what you need to overcome your own obstacles and succeed in your own life. In doing so, you'll become your own version of a Poly-Esther.

CHAPTER FIFTEEN
The Friendship Maker

My mother never got a college education. Although we shared a first name—Esther—she chose a very different path. She raised eight children in all. When she married my father, he was widowed and had four children of his own. His first wife died giving birth. My mother raised those four children and had four more.

Though she didn't have a long list of educational titles to her name, my mother had so much wisdom! My siblings and I fought it during our growing years, but over time, we grew to respect her greatly. She taught us many things through her example.

In this chapter, I'll take some time to reflect on the lessons my mother demonstrated in her daily life. She set an example of surrounding yourself with others and finding the sunshine through the rain. In my own life and friendships today, I aim to emulate her standards. If you strive to do the same, I can assure you it will help you get through the bad times. And for those good times? You'll have someone (or many someones!) to celebrate them with you.

A Nod to Everyone

One of the main things I've learned from my mother that I will always treasure and try to apply in my own life is to respect all people. As a child in Puerto Rico, if I were walking with my mother down the street in town, it seemed like she knew everybody. We would pass a homeless person asking for money, and she would greet them by name. Then we might walk a little further and see the mayor of the town. Guess what? She was on a first-name basis with the mayor, too. And she would say "hello" to both in the same manner.

She treated everybody the same, and she was well respected in town for it. Later in her life she received an award from the town where she lived. The recognition was for being such a service to the community. She had friends of all ages, and any "differences" were unknown to her.

My mother lived in Puerto Rico her entire life. When she passed away, one of my sisters who lives there planned the funeral. I flew from the United States to attend the service.

I was astounded by the number of people who came to the viewing. So many people showed up in fact that my sister had to extend the hours of the viewing. It was such an expression of who our mother was and how she treated others.

That day, I had young men and women come up to me and say, "Your mother was my best friend! I am going to miss her so much!" I also had older ladies approach me and say, "You know, your mother meant so much to me. She was my best friend."

My mother knew how to surround herself with people, and make everyone in her midst feel like they mattered. She really cared about others, and she cast a wide net. She made friends easily and people always remembered her. Her funeral was a fitting reminder of the friendships she nurtured throughout her life.

Learning from Each Other

Now as an adult, I try to cast a wide net, like my mother did. I have some friends who I know I can count on when I need a good listener. I can turn to them and be sure that they will not judge me. They won't interrupt me, no matter how long I talk! When I finally finish, they often share great insights that make me feel better. They know they don't have to solve my problems; I am always grateful to simply have their ear.

Then there are the friends who are the movers and the shakers. If I need a rally cry to charge ahead, they will form the ranks and offer to run with me. They love action and aren't afraid of conflict. This is a vital group of friends to have, as they help motivate me to sort out issues and forge onward.

I could go on, as I have a wide range of social circles (like my mother did). The great part of diversity is that everyone brings something to the table. People who have achieved high levels of success bring a perspective of experience. Those that just switched industries might have a fresh set of eyes as they survey my niche. They may be able to share insights they learned during their time in a different market segment.

At each level, we can lean into others, regardless of where they are in life. I always say there's no need to reject people just because they happen to be in a different phase of life. You know what my current favorite age is? Preschoolers! My grandchildren who are young help me stay creative and remember what it's like to play and imagine.

Mixing the Generations

While I joke that I have to make friends with younger people because the older generation is passing away, I didn't invent the saying. Any guesses on where I first heard it? If you answered, "Your mother," you are correct. My mother not only stated this; she lived it. When she was in her sixties, she made friends with others in their twenties and thirties.

She even explained this to me once: "You know my best friends? All of them are either my age or older … and you know what? They're dying. So my new strategy is that I'm gonna get friends that are twenty or thirty years younger than me so I don't run out of friends."

My mother was such a character! Yet I find myself doing the same thing now. I regularly get together with others who are just starting their career. We go out for coffee, or I have them over for dinner. I also maintain groups of friends who are my peers and get along with those who are older than me.

There are so many benefits to this strategy that can be applied to the workplace. The idea is a bit of a countertrend to what many companies lean toward doing. It's not uncommon to overlook older workers, or to offer early retirement packages as a way to incentivize them to step down from their positions. Some of them have spent the last decades in their respective careers. Many older workers find it difficult to get a new job, especially if they have been asked to leave their previous employer.

For those that stay, they may face ageism and criticism. Seniors in a work environment that favors younger employees will likely get passed over when it is time to grant promotions. They may be handed projects that don't align with their areas of expertise. They might feel left out, especially if conversations focus on young family needs or the nightlife scene for singles.

On top of these fluctuations lies an overarching trend. This shift relates to the length of time that the new generations stay at their workplace. More and more, younger people are not as loyal to one employer. Gone are the days of working for a firm for thirty years and then taking a pension. I've seen folks get tired after two years—or less—especially if they don't see a chance for growth. This younger generation tends to jump from one place to another.

Putting this all together, I see several opportunities for companies that want to retain their strong employees. While not everyone will want the chance to become a director or CEO, some will specifically look for ways to be challenged and to grow. (I know I certainly did throughout my career!) If there is a path for top talent to follow so they can become leaders, and an employee development program is implemented, companies could find that their best workers stay with them.

Drawing on this further, we could effectively have a new group dynamic. Senior employees with years of experience could share their knowledge with the younger workers. These new team members, for their part, could learn what to do—and what to avoid.

So often we have this gap between the generations, and if we work to include a diversity of ages, we could fill that space. In fact, one of the best well-kept secrets among the centennial regions of the world is that the older generation never loses their role in society. They always feel that they have a place and are valued. This arrangement benefits the entire society, as the younger people can learn from the older ones. Certainly, I am not advocating for eliminating early retirement or retirement. I am advocating for valuing diversity of ages as to maximize leveraging experience and new technology. If this is done effectively, we could have a mix of younger and older team members who could support each other while in the workplace together.

These concepts really stem from my mother's example. She knew how to interact with people of all ages, and she cherished all of her relationships. People replicated the care and concern she showed to them. Perhaps the best lesson she can teach us all is that everyone craves respect. When we give it, we can be ready to reap rewards tenfold—or more.

Questions for Reflection

- Do you regularly interact with different age groups? How has this impacted you?
- Are there opportunities in your workplace to encourage mixing generations?
- What have older individuals in your life taught you? Have you found examples you'd like to follow?
- What changes would you like to make in your life to improve your intergenerational relationships?

CHAPTER SIXTEEN
The Mirror

By nature, I am usually willing to share my own experiences with others. When someone tells me they are struggling with something, my heart goes out to them. After I hear about their problems, I'm generally ready to open my own book. It's typically the way that I mentor and coach others.

Here's the thing: people are often surprised to hear what I have gone through (perhaps you have been startled at certain times during this book too!). At the same time, they usually appreciate it when I share my background with them. Perhaps it gives them hope that they too will see a better day.

I want to look at some of the ways I've used my own experiences to help others. I regularly mentor up-and-coming professionals, and it gives me great joy to see them advance and even flourish. If I can play a role in helping them get to the next point in their career, for me, it's worth it. Even if that means I have to share some of my less-than-glamorous past to help them move up.

Seeking the Sunshine

Although I tend to follow the principles of letting others know what I've gone through, there have been certain moments that I kept to myself for a period. My mental health challenges, for instance, were ones that I couldn't talk about initially. Perhaps it was because I was raised during a different time—when I grew up, no one around me talked about depression. It was something that everyone seemed to ignore, or at least not know very much about. Whatever the reason, I felt like if I shared, people wouldn't understand. Instead, I would be put aside.

After my diagnosis, I even fought doctors on the idea of telling my story to others. I was first treated in a hospital in the Southeast, and my doctor there monitored my medicine after I left. While I was encouraged to try therapy in addition to the drugs, I wasn't that interested. I preferred to surround myself with others who were doing well.

When I moved to Hawaii, a similar scene played out. I found a psychiatrist there who could continue to watch over my condition. I saw her frequently, as I had to have sessions with her so she could renew the prescription. She talked to me about my life and how I was doing. She was really proud of me and how far I had come. At that point, I was in college, maintaining good grades, and nourishing my growing children. I hadn't fallen into episodes of depression that sent me back into the hospital. Instead, I was improving over time and felt more positive about life.

One day, when I met with the psychiatrist, she started talking to me like she usually did. Then she changed the topic and started telling me about a support group. She said she was running group therapy sessions for people going through depression and mental health challenges. She went on to add that she thought I would make such a good example for other people going through the same type of experience. She asked me to join the group. She wanted me to share with them what I had gone through and how I overcame it.

I listened to her and when she finished, I didn't respond right away. Then I told her what I knew I wanted in my heart. I said, "No."

She was fairly taken aback by my answer (like I said I am full of surprises!). I went on to explain that I didn't want to surround myself with people who were going through the same thing. "I cannot," I added. "I don't want to talk—it doesn't do me good."

The psychiatrist was starting to understand where I was coming from. "What I want to talk about is activities," I continued, "and actions that we're going to take. But I don't want to talk about dark things—that's why I have you! I pay you for that."

Sharing My Struggles

That conversation took place during my mid-twenties. I kept my mental health history and medication to myself and my doctor for the following decades. There were a few exceptions of course. And after I started dating Carlos, I knew he would eventually learn that I took a pill every day to maintain my mental health. I decided to be upfront and told him about the medication for my depression. I wasn't sure how he would react. I was startled when he responded, "You are the most well, emotionally stable person that I have seen." He continued, "I know a lot of people that are not emotionally stable, and they supposedly don't have any mental issues." Fortunately, he has always supported me, and I appreciate that.

It wasn't until I reached my sixties that I found it easier to share. As I did, I realized that others might benefit from hearing my tale. This was particularly true with one connection I made in Hawaii.

Several years ago, I was asked to speak to the graduate students at the university I attended in Hawaii. I wanted to go to the island and connect with the advisors I had during my years in the doctorate program. I agreed to give a presentation for the doctoral students who had completed their studies.

To prepare, I put together some slides with images on them. I chose pictures of a mountain, then a wall, and finally the stairs. I knew the analogy would help guide my speech and remind me of what to say—that their climb to the top might feel like having to get to the peak, only to face a barrier to break down, and finally climb up, step by step.

When it was time to present, the slides seemed to resonate with the graduates in front of me. Afterward, many of them came up to me and asked questions. Some of them wanted to connect on LinkedIn, and I agreed. I encouraged them to reach out to me if they had any questions.

Sometime later, out of the blue, I received an email. It was from one of the attendees at the graduate student talk I gave in Hawaii. He began, "I don't know if you remember me, but I'm a student and I heard your talk. You told me I could reach out to you if I needed anything. And I would like some help."

After reading his note, I responded that I was open to meeting with him. We scheduled a video chat, and he began to tell me his story. He mentioned that he was a PhD student and that he had started writing his dissertation. He knew he would need to defend it. And then he started finding it difficult to talk. He broke down a little, almost crying.

When he gained control of his words again, he stated that he felt he couldn't finish and defend the dissertation. He was battling depression and anxiety, and he didn't think he would be able to talk in front of people. He was blocked even just thinking about being in front of people, not to mention the PhD board members.

As I listened to him, I couldn't help but think about my own time on the island, decades before. I had been older than the other PhD students; I had been given such a hard time during my presentations that I cried after them; I had been told I shouldn't do the program because I was a parent ... and on and on. I also remembered how I had finished all the courses, completed the dissertation, *defended it*, and gone on to have a career.

Even as those thoughts ran through my head, I let the young PhD student finish. Then I calmly said, "You know, this is an opportunity for me to share and be open. I will tell you about some hard things I went through. I hope that as you hear my story, it helps you in some way."

I then said that I didn't plan in life to have anxiety and clinical depression. "But it happened to me." I went on, "You know, for a long time I struggled to understand this, and it took years for me to process it. Even today I have to use treatment, and when I need to I have my doctor that I trust."

I am pretty sure he wasn't expecting me to share that I had a similar condition! To put it in perspective, I said, "You know, it's become an aspect of my life that I have and manage. It's really no different from a condition like diabetes. We have to monitor it and decide to go on with life."

Through sharing my own experiences, I was telling him that he wasn't alone. After relaying my story, I laid out some of the things he could work on. I reviewed his fear of speaking in front of people and how he would get very nervous just at the thought of standing up.

Then I suggested we look for something to do about those hesitancies. I encouraged him to think about how to conquer them. I mentioned that finding a tool or setting a goal might help him overcome the issue. I also assured him that I get nervous every time I have to talk in front of people, and that those feelings are normal.

At the end of our conversation, I suggested he think about practicing in front of others. I also offered to be the person he could use to test out his presentation. "Also when it's time to do the real thing, maybe you want to unfocus your eyes on the committee. You could try to trick your brain into thinking, 'I am in a room by myself.' And by the way, you're speaking very well right now, so you definitely have the skill for it. But we cannot let a health issue dominate your life."

It is my hope that these young people, like the struggling PhD student, see the light. That there is always a way through, even when the way seems foggy at times. I know I found it hard during my twenties and thirties to find the sunshine. I'm glad I hung on—and that's why I want to help others complete the ride too.

Questions for Reflection

- Have you ever talked to someone and assumed they were successful from day 1 of their lives? How did that make you feel?
- What experiences might you share with others who are going through a difficult time? Have you been through challenges that have taught you significant lessons?
- How might talking to a mentor help you sort issues and make a plan to move forward?
- What value can come from being open and vulnerable among friends and coworkers?

CHAPTER SEVENTEEN
The Poly-Esther

I may have retired from certain stages of my career (specifically working for large biopharma companies), but I recently founded and took the role of CEO for APIE Therapeutics, a new biopharma start-up with the goal of developing new drug therapies for rare diseases. Sometimes when I felt down about the business I was leading, such as after a long string of "No's" when asking for funding, I would tell my husband to buy a baseball bat. I shared this with others too. I pleaded with everyone in my circle of close friends and family to purchase a baseball bat.

When they asked me, "Why?" (and they always do), I gave an answer. This response was always the same. I told them that if they ever heard me talking about founding and starting a new biopharma company, I wanted them to go grab that bat. Then I wanted them to beat me with it until I couldn't move.

They thought I was crazy.

But I wasn't finished. I explained that I wanted to be reminded that this was the hardest challenge I had ever taken on. I didn't want to talk myself into beginning another.

All joking aside, I'll be the first to admit that it's tough to lead a new company. Even though I recently moved to a new role as innovation officer, there have been times when I have wanted to quit, even though I knew I had made it through other obstacles in the past. I have also been told that the current climate makes it especially difficult. In a fluctuating market with uncertain economic predictions, investors are typically more hesitant to offer support. Throw in the fact that we're working on providing treatments for rare medical conditions, as opposed to therapies for mainstream ailments which might draw more attention, and you may understand the reasoning behind my baseball bat pounding request.

Still, I think there are lessons in this feeling that can serve us all. This endeavor of a start-up has given me the opportunity to reflect on where I'm at—and where I began. It's caused me to realize that reaching this milestone of being a founder and CEO and building the company structure from bottom up was beyond my imagination for so long. After three years, we brought on board a new CEO and I took the role of chief innovation officer to see through to completion several collaborations we established with the National Institutes of Health and other well-known research institutions.

The Mountain, Wall, and Stairs

Decades ago, I never would have dreamed of getting to this point. If you would have told my teenage self that I would be leading a company and mentoring others on the side, I never would have believed you. The same is true for the twenty-something-year-old version of me. I thought it was impossible. At the time, I didn't even have a four-year degree. Plus, I had growing children and a family to look after.

Getting to where I am today took a great deal of time, and I accumulated many experiences as I traveled along the path to arrive at the life I have today. Now, as I reflect, I can better see how these moments collectively helped me develop self-esteem. They also allowed me to see higher-up roles and responsibilities. Once I viewed these, I found increased motivation to take on more assignments, give my all, and form my own future.

Building Self-Esteem

With my past and childhood, there were definitely times when I doubted myself. I didn't grow up in a household where self-confidence was encouraged. I felt surrounded by others who were better in some way than me (and maybe you can relate: insert a word here such as "smarter" or "more charming"). I was always a step behind others in so many areas of life.

But then something happens. Through hard work and persistence, maybe you reach a small goal. That might be getting a job, finishing college, or gaining a promotion. If you are rewarded for your efforts or receive a special recognition, it can be especially meaningful. You might feel a boost in your self-worth. Those doubts about failure that always seem so close to your head and heart may start to fade a bit.

I know that for me, reaching these achievements proved valuable for my own self-esteem. In some cases, I thought those milestones were so far out of reach that I could hardly accept them to be true. It was really engrained in me that I was slated for second. I always worked hard and gave my best—that I knew. But I didn't carry out those efforts with a goal of being promoted or looking for recognition. I figured the baton would be passed to others. And it often was, which further instilled my apprehension about moving up.

This perspective led to some hilarious moments in the workplace. One time, my supervisor called me into his office. I figured he wanted to talk to me about some issue, though I wasn't sure which one. When the two of us were alone in his office, he closed the door. *Here it comes,* I thought. I wondered which work challenge in my department we were going to be discussing.

Instead of bringing up a problem, he shared with me the news that I was getting promoted. The statement left me speechless. I didn't know how to respond. In fact, I was so surprised to be promoted that I started looking around the room, certain that my supervisor was talking to someone else. I checked behind the curtains and under the desk. "What are you doing?" he finally asked me.

"Looking to see who is here, who you want to promote," I replied.

"It's you," he assured me.

Moments like that were life-changing for me. Certainly, they marked a change in my work duties and daily tasks. More than that, however, they boosted my self-esteem. I went from having very low self-esteem to gaining confidence—and it really helped that others saw something in me that I didn't seem to recognize.

Over time, these developments added up. Looking back, I can think of big moments, like college graduation, getting a PhD, being promoted to a manager, then a director, then the executive level, to vice president. I became a board member, a chairperson of boards, a founder, a CEO, a chief innovation officer. Each title and landmark are filed away inside of me. I may not list them to others in my life every day, but they are still there. They helped me to believe that I really could do something, and that I could reach the next level.

Each of these holds its own significance in this chain, in this Poly-Esther that I have become. They each mark a point in time when I grew, and in this sense, they represent achievements of all sizes. As they come together, I can be sure that the new entity they are forming is stronger than what I had in the past.

Flying the Airplane

I remember feeling so proud of myself when I finished my bachelor's degree. Here I was, graduating alongside others who were twenty-one or twenty-two years old. I was twenty-seven. I could have felt down about the timing. But instead, I was so happy—it was an accomplishment that I had only dreamed of in my early twenties. Finishing a bachelor's degree was a big deal for me.

Then I started the next dream, which involved being part of a company in the innovation side of pharmaceuticals. It meant I had to get the PhD and complete the post-doc work too. Once I completed those and was hired at an organization, I didn't start in a director role. I worked as a team member, which was exciting to me at the time. I got to be exposed to scientists and learn from them. The environment was so different from my years of college, as there were no quizzes and tests to take every week. But I had the chance to learn about management and see who was making the decisions. With this information, I was able to visualize what I wanted to be next in my career.

This trajectory was a bit like flying an airplane. In the pilot's seat, you can only see what is in front of you. It may be a specific point you are trying to reach. Once you get that far, you begin to see a new view. You start to think about that next destination and accomplishment.

I remember meeting people in leadership roles and thinking, *I would love to be in his position! And I want to have that leadership style too.* In my case, I always emulated traits that portrayed an openness. I wanted everyone to find me approachable. I think part of me never let go to those feelings of being left behind, of laying at the bottom, of not being in the airplane. Once I had others tell me I was doing a good job, pull me up, and place me into the cockpit, I found it easier to think of more possibilities for my future.

As the conversations shifted from being operational to taking on a strategic tone, I continued to learn. And they made me dream of what could be next. I could visualize where I wanted to be. Then I could look for opportunities to reach that next goal.

That pattern has followed me all these years. When I founded APIE Therapeutics, I ventured into new territory once again. Suddenly I had to be involved in fund-raising efforts, which was something I had never done before. While I had fought for budgets and managed them at other companies, this scene was new. It consisted of reaching out to venture capitalists and investors. I would need to give presentations and show them there was value in supporting the start-up company.

To help me get through, I began visualizing what I wanted to achieve. I would close my eyes and see myself standing in front of a group of investors and biopharma leaders. They would be signing an agreement that stated their commitment to provide funding to take our drug development to clinical trials. I would be accepting their offer, and so pleased that we had the funding we needed to move forward.

Like the other dreams in the past, this vision at times seemed impossible. I received so many "No's" that I lost count. Some potential investors told me that our area of therapeutics is not within their scope of investments. Others stated that I came too early—they need to see successful clinical trials to commit. I had leaders tell me, "I love the science, and I love the team. I think you are awesome … but we can only invest if you have human data."

One of the board members of our company, a physician by training, could always sense when I had received a long string of bad news. Perhaps he empathized with me because he's been in my shoes before, having been involved in various ventures and start-ups. He always seemed to sense when I was feeling down. We might have a tough board meeting, and I would find it hard to hide the strain. I most likely looked weary and beaten. In these instances, it wouldn't be unusual for him to call me after the discussion ended and everyone went home. He seemed to have a sixth sense about these issues.

"Esther," he would begin. "How are you doing?"

After some small talk, he would get to his point. "I have done this, and I know what you're going through. It's very tough. What you need to do today is get a big bottle of wine and serve yourself a nice glass. Take the rest of the day off, pour yourself a second large glass of wine, and enjoy it. And then have one more glass."

I would always thank him for his advice. Then I would add, "There's just one problem. I don't drink!"

Playing into my humor, he would reply, "Well, I guess you have to start—if you want to survive!"

I appreciated the gesture every time. It helps to know that others support you, especially during the difficult times. It's also a good reminder to take a break when you need it, and then dive back into the challenges at hand. In the case of the start-up, I know that we have to push through the hard times—and all the "No's"—to get through to the eventual "Yes" and light at the end of the tunnel.

Driving me, as before, is the commitment to be involved in innovation and help patients who are in need of better treatments. Sometimes after a hard day, I just have to remember my conversations with the patients we want to help. They have shared with me details about their disease and day-to-day struggles. I recall that most of what they get prescribed is to address a symptom but not the cause of the disease so they never feel better and their disease continues to progress. After I recall these conversations, I am always ready to get to work again on finding them a solution that can better their outcome.

Regarding the challenges of my start-up, I know that this is not the first time I have wanted to run. There were other times in my career when I held leadership positions at companies and wanted to escape. Sometimes there were issues that came up that were out of my control, like supply chain problems. And I still had to perform. So I tell that to myself on the tough days that I still need to move forward.

And after three years in the role of founder and CEO, we raised enough funding to take the first drug therapy for systemic sclerosis to a pre-IND meeting with the FDA. We also have a pipeline for other therapeutic areas, including kidney disease and metabolic syndrome. The company has an outstanding board of directors and scientific advisors. Most recently, we brought on a new CEO to drive the next level of growth for the company. I certainly feel proud that I had the chance to again dive into the unknown and learn valuable new lessons, while expanding into meeting so many wonderful professionals.

Who knows? I might just do another start-up! The bat, please?

Questions for Reflection

- Have you taken on challenges that seem to have no end in sight? How did you get through them?
- Do you find it helpful to reflect on how far you've come when you're feeling down? Why or why not?
- What goal could you try visualizing? What would your life look like if you reached it?
- How might you help someone else who is going through a hard time? Imagine what you might say and how you might act around them.

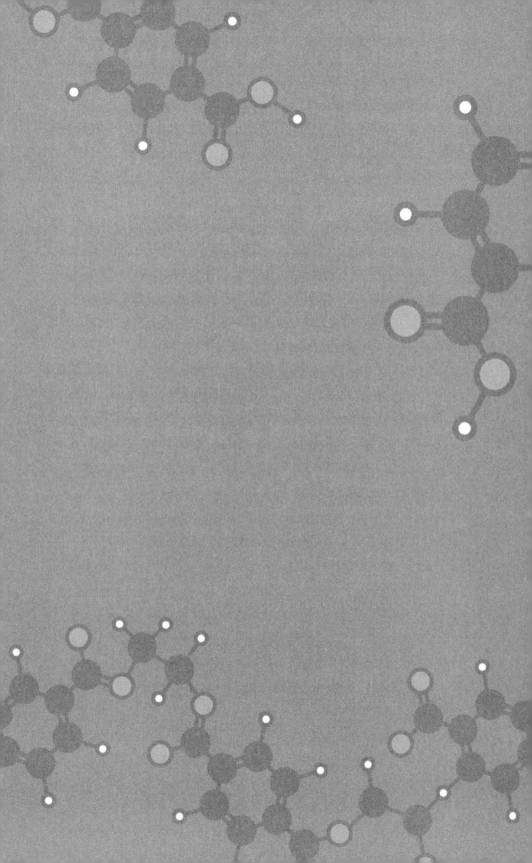

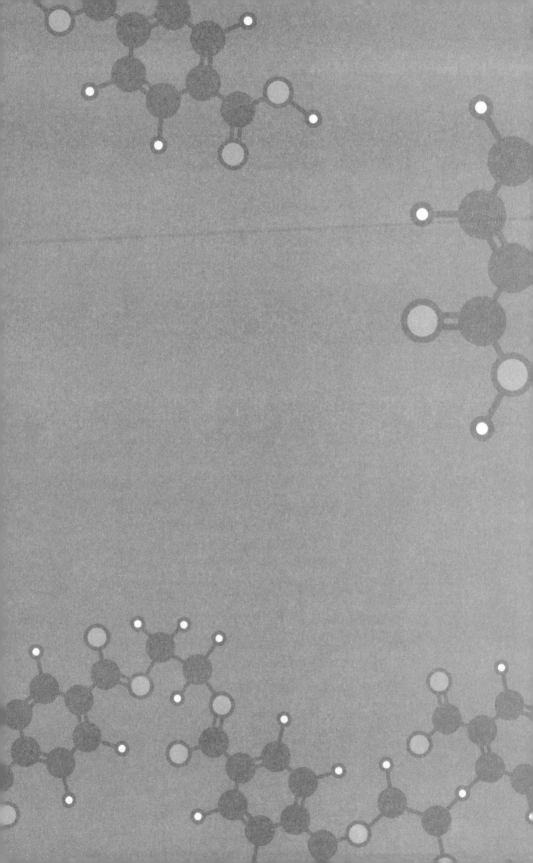

CONCLUSION
The Unretired

"When are you going to retire?"

"Are you thinking about retirement yet?"

I have been asked these questions and others like them many times over the years. They are typically innocent inquiries, asked by those I know who are curious about the next steps I'll take. They want to know my plans.

But over the years, I've learned that there's really not such a thing as retirement. Instead, the concept involves more of a movement. You go from one journey to another. This is especially true if you are someone who gets stimulated by learning and challenging yourself. In my case, as we've seen in the previous chapters, I definitely am always looking for the next opportunity to grow and develop. It doesn't bother me to be pushed out of my comfort zone.

That's why, rather than moving away from continuing to learn and challenge myself and settling away from impacting innovation in therapeutic drug discovery, I've found myself taking other paths. There have been chances to give back, to build, and to help others. Those endeavors continue to pull me up in the morning and drive me to continue striving forward. Don't get me wrong—spending some time at the seashore and traveling the world learning about other cultures has its appeal as well, and I carve out vacation time to do so. However, I've found that I'm at my best when I'm hard at work learning in some capacity.

When I first considered stepping away from my position as an executive, I knew I would be able to do so financially. I had saved over the years, and every single promotion or bonus I had received had been readily stashed away. As a result of this diligence, there was a cushion that could support me, meaning that I wouldn't have to search for a part-time gig or different role out of need.

At the time, I spotted a shift in the company that aligned with my thoughts of doing something else. I had worked hard for decades and wondered if it was time to pursue other efforts. I was looking at a move as well, from cold Boston back to North Carolina, and it seemed appropriate to reduce my workload by "retiring" from the company.

It would be just that: I knew I was leaving one organization. I would find another—and this time, since I wasn't financially driven, I was free to consider an assortment of places. I started my search and asked the question, "Where can I help?"

Don't worry, I soon found opportunities! (As my husband Carlos says, "You have two velocities: you are either running or sleeping!") I encountered a free medical clinic that operated as a nonprofit. I was asked to become a board member of the organization, and I felt that I could draw on my background and experience to add value. I accepted the offer and started attending meetings. This was my first foray into something different—it wasn't a full-time job or a promotion within my career.

However, it still brought a level of excitement that I loved. As I got more involved in the nonprofit world, I could see that changes were underway in the area where the organization was operating. The population was growing, and yet the nonprofit lacked a vision to set the course to continue to assist their increasing numbers. I asked about this, gathered data related to the region and its numbers, and encouraged them to set a long-term goal. As a result of my efforts, I was asked to be chairperson of the board of directors! This soon became a very involved project, and I spent countless hours immersed in it.

So much for my "retirement"! In all honesty, I often like to avoid the word "retirement." It conveys a sense of a stage being over, and an ending. I prefer to look at it as a step toward something else. That's exactly the course my "retirement" has taken. Perhaps that's why it didn't bother me that I dedicated so much time to the nonprofit—it was more of what I had in mind for this point in my life, and I am grateful that I have been able to follow this path of helping others.

In addition to serving as chairperson of that nonprofit, I have also been asked to participate on other boards. Each of these opportunities has allowed me the chance to give back and help in a certain way. I have been able to offer insight into government-assisted efforts, to public boards, and to private arenas.

I love the dynamic of the boards I am on. Rather than the steep competition that was so prominent throughout my career, as many fought their way to the top and even pushed down others to get there, these meetings are full of experts who have already established themselves in their respective industries. The other board members tend to respect one another's opinion and accept the insight each person brings. Collectively we can work together to spot areas for improvement and growth. It really seems like a team effort, and I'm happy to be part of that.

Perhaps you might say that I have enjoyed these boards so much I started my company to have one of my own! Being a founder, CEO, and chief innovation officer of a start-up with goals to develop new therapeutic drugs and deliver them to the market may be the biggest challenge I've taken on so far, but I have no regrets. My passion to help others and improve patient outcomes, which really instigated my whole career, continues to drive me each and every day.

But always there is the special joy I find in extending a hand to others who are looking for a brighter future and career. I have faced everything from abuse to divorce to single parenthood, mental health challenges, immigration and language barriers, educational obstacles, and more—and I've made it through.

That mountain, wall, and staircase I used in a presentation? They are challenges that you can get through, too. No matter where you are, if you look for opportunities, you will find one. I've seen it done before. And I'm here to help you if you're looking for advice (or just another fun story—we will laugh together!). I see mentoring interwoven into the journey of my life, as I continue to travel down the road. One thing is for sure: I'm always looking for companions! And those who are younger than me don't bother me in the least—as I tell my children, I need more people in my life who are decades or more behind me, so they can be around and keep me company for many years to come!

And what I've learned most along the way is that at every point, you get to grow a little. These mini developments become a part of who you are. Eventually they all link together ... and you become that poly-version of yourself. It is my hope that when you get to that point, you'll be able to look back and see just how far you've come. And know that you've become a Poly-John or a Poly-Carmella, with your many different traits linking to form an entity that is uniquely, only, you.

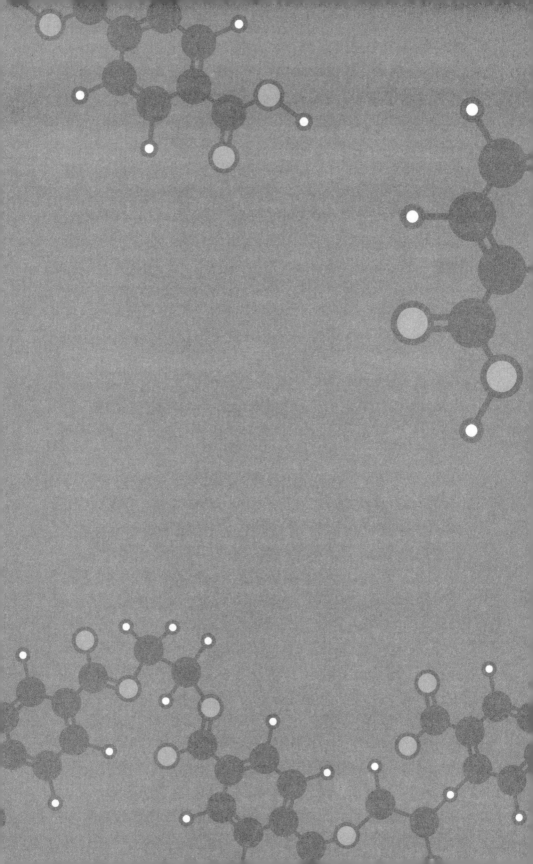

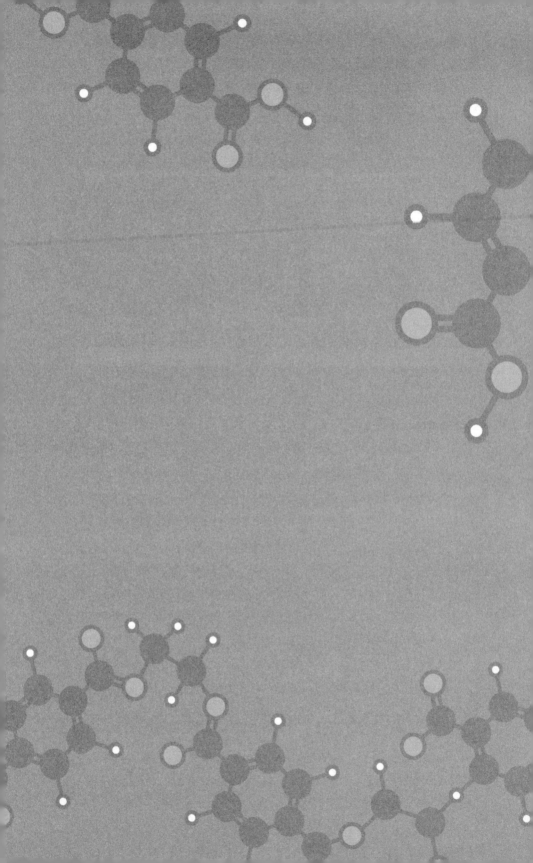

ABOUT THE AUTHOR

With more than three decades in the biopharmaceuticals industry, Dr. Esther M. Alegria has overseen strategic and operational initiatives in Europe, the United States, and Puerto Rico. As the founder and chief innovation officer of APIE Therapeutics, based in the Research Triangle Park in North Carolina, Dr. Alegria is a leader in developing therapeutic drugs to treat chronic and debilitating diseases. Throughout her career, Dr. Alegria has been passionate about improving health outcomes for patients. She willingly draws on her experience and expertise to mentor professionals and students. She also serves on several boards, including the board of directors for Avid Bioservices, the board of directors for STERIS, and the board of trustees for the PR Science Trust. Dr. Alegria holds a PhD in chemistry from the University of Hawaii and an executive business management certification from Harvard Business School. Originally from Puerto Rico, Dr. Alegria now resides in Cary, North Carolina.

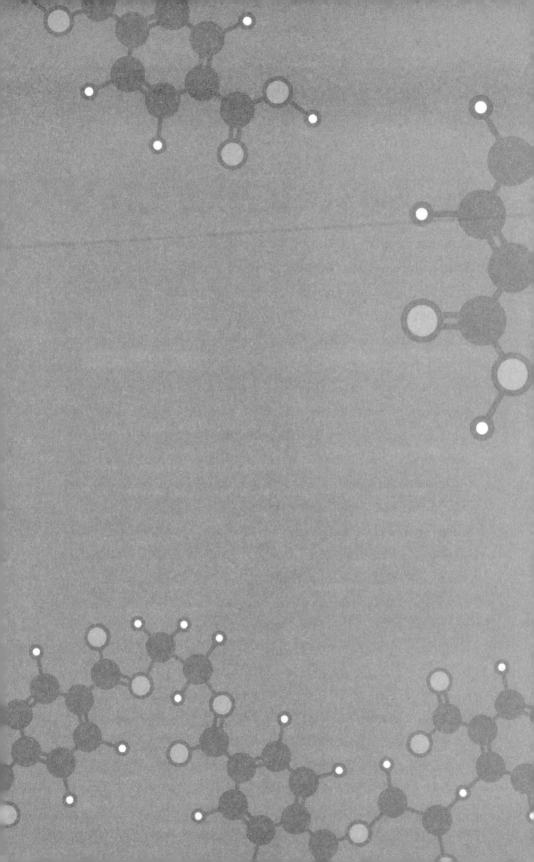

ACKNOWLEDGMENTS

I wouldn't be here (in so many ways) without the important examples that my grandmother, Amalia Rolon-Rivera, and mother, Esther Alicea-Rolon, set for me. Born in 1905 and 1930, respectively, they didn't receive a lot of education, but their work ethic and the values they portrayed were incredible. They lived and moved during a different era; still, their legacy and teachings remain relevant today.

I want to acknowledge Dr. Chia-Lung Hsieh, my first professional mentor when I joined Wyeth as a research scientist. He was a role model for me as a leader of people. He was always open to mentoring me, spoke up for me in front of others, and took initiatives to elevate me to the next level. Though he has passed away, he is always in my heart.

A special nod goes to John Cox, my foremost mentor at Biogen, who was able to see beyond my appearance and accent, and empowered me to take chances outside my comfort zone—ultimately promoting me to be the first woman to serve as vice president of manufacturing.